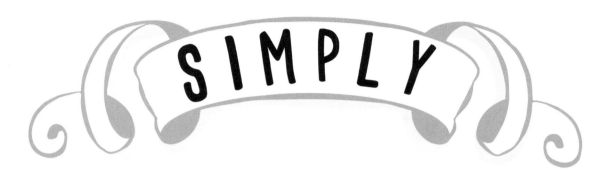

SIMPLY

TRADITION

70 FUN & EASY HOLIDAY IDEAS FOR FAMILIES

For my darling family . . . they are everything to me.
Rick, Ryan, Kate, Emma, Henry, Jack, and Caroline

For my parents, who gave me a wonderful
childhood full of tradition.

ISBN: 978-1-4621-1922-6

Published by Plain Sight Publishing, an imprint of Cedar Fort, Inc.
2373 W. 700 S., Springville, UT, 84663
Distributed by Cedar Fort, Inc., www.cedarfort.com

LIBRARY OF CONGRESS CATALOGING-IN-PUBLICATION DATA

Names: Wade, Kierste, 1975- author.
Title: Simply tradition / Kierste Wade.
Description: Springville, Utah : Plain Sight Publishing, an imprint of Cedar
    Fort, Inc., [2016] | Includes bibliographical references and index.
Identifiers: LCCN 2016022611 (print) | LCCN 2016024083 (ebook) | ISBN
    9781462119226 (perfect bound : alk. paper) | ISBN 9781462127030 (epub,
    pdf, and mobi)
Subjects: LCSH: Families--United States. | United States--Social life and
    customs. | Holidays--United States.
Classification: LCC GT2420 .W33 2016 (print) | LCC GT2420 (ebook) | DDC
    390.0973--dc23
LC record available at https://lccn.loc.gov/2016022611

Cover design by Kinsey Beckett
Page design by Priscilla Chaves
Cover design © 2016 Cedar Fort, Inc.
Edited by Jessica Romrell

Printed in the United States of America

10 9 8 7 6 5 4 3 2 1

Printed on acid-free paper

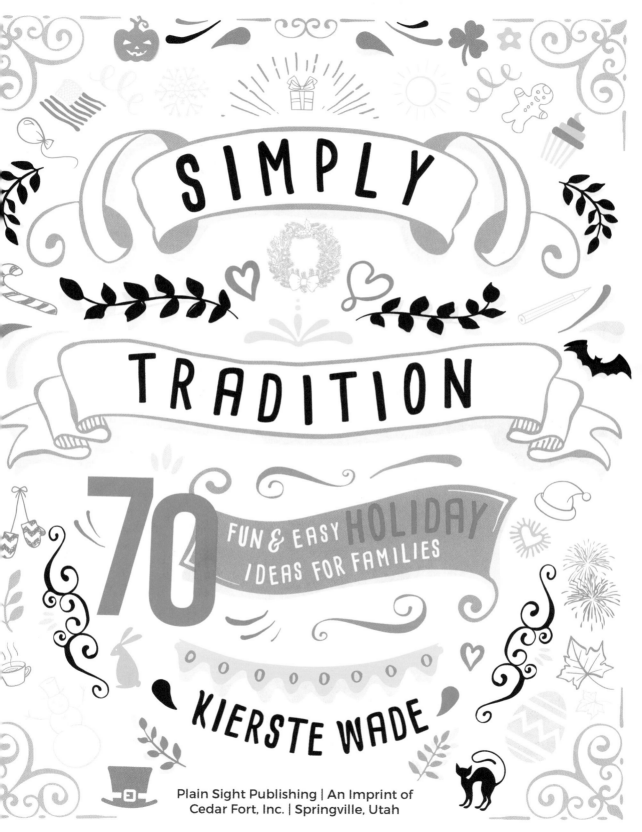

SIMPLY
TRADITION

70 FUN & EASY HOLIDAY IDEAS FOR FAMILIES

KIERSTE WADE

Plain Sight Publishing | An Imprint of
Cedar Fort, Inc. | Springville, Utah

INTRODUCTION

My daughter was about five years old when I discovered she knew what a tradition was. She may not have known the actual word, but she knew what it meant to her, and how it made her feel. We were talking about the upcoming holiday, and she mentioned that she couldn't wait for one particular activity. I asked her how she knew that's what we would be doing, and she just looked at me and replied, "because that's what we always do!" And she was right.

Tradition is a big part of our family life all year, especially during the holidays. I know for our family, having traditions has such a positive impact on our lives. When I think about all the things we look forward to during the year, and when I ask my kids about what they are looking forward to, inevitably it's the things that we do every year—our traditions—that are at the top of the list.

According to the Merriam-Webster dictionary, one of the definitions of tradition is:

"the handing down of information, beliefs, and customs by word of mouth or by example from one generation to another without written instruction"

My own definition of a tradition is simplified even more—it's basically anything that your family does together on regular basis. There is no right or wrong, no certain way a tradition needs to be or should be done. It doesn't have to be fancy or take a lot of preparation, although it's okay if it does. It's simply a family spending time together doing something they enjoy. Don't worry about creating the "perfect" family tradition—perfection isn't in the activity itself, it's just the outcome of being together. What it comes down to is spending time together as family—creating memories, strengthening relationships, celebrating the holidays we love and hold dear—together.

Holiday traditions are important because they connect us to the past, are a bridge to the future, and create strong family bonds. They also give us a sense of belonging, and help us celebrate generations of family. Traditions build memories, and they hold a very strong place in our hearts. Some of my earliest memories are of traditions not only with my parents, but also with my grandparents.

I love traditions all year long, but most especially at the holidays. They foster excitement as we celebrate each holiday, make them more meaningful, and give us the opportunity to share something special with all the members of our family. In this busy world, traditions are what slow it down a little, and provide us a reason and an opportunity to do so.

As I spoke with people about their family traditions, I often got the response that "we do same things that everyone else does," inferring that their traditions might not be as special, or as important because of it. Yes, on Christmas morning there are a lot of families opening gifts, yet if you could peek inside each one, you would never find two houses doing it the same way, because there aren't two families that are the same.

If you don't have a rich history of tradition, that's okay—not every family does. It just gives you the opportunity and freedom to start your own. It's never too late to start or add new traditions! Some traditions come about as a matter of circumstance—something that "just happened" one year and then it's carried over. Others are intentional. But no matter how or when they're started, they will enrich and deepen your family's holiday experiences and your relationships with each other.

I am thrilled to be sharing with you our family's favorite holiday traditions from throughout the year. We love them, and they've brought much happiness to our home. I hope that whether you adopt them into your family or use them as a catalyst for your own ideas, you will find meaning and joy as you celebrate the holidays with your family.

From our home to yours . . . happy holidays!

TABLE OF CONTENTS

SECTION THREE: WINTER

SECTION FOUR: SPRING

SECTION FIVE: SUMMER

BACK-TO-SCHOOL COUNTDOWN

There's a lot of enthusiasm around our house for the first day of school. The kids wait not so patiently for the letters from school to come, telling them which teacher they'll have for the next year, and they can't wait to compare notes with their friends to see who's in their class. We're scooping up school supplies, planning first-day-of-school outfits, and deciding what to pack in lunches. We're always sad to say good-bye to the carefree summer after enjoying all the freedoms it's offered us, but the appeal of the school year, getting back into a routine, and the impending fall season is so exciting.

Our family loves countdowns, and we use them to look forward to all kinds of things—holidays, trips, the days until dad comes home from a business trip—and no matter what the countdown is for, it works to not only build excitement, but help us (me) plan. Not only for school starting, but also for all of the things we want to make sure and do before the summer is over.

A couple of years ago, I created this fun chalkboard back-to-school countdown, and it was a huge hit. My kids especially loved the washi tape part of things, and each day, they took turns choosing the color they wanted, and place it on the next number. I clipped it up on my refrigerator, and it was a fun reminder of how many days were left before school started again!

• • • • • •

PRINTING INSTRUCTIONS

Enter the following URL in the address bar of your computer, and save. Upload it to the photo center of your choice (or save it to a flash drive and take it in) to be printed as an 8 x 10 photo.

bit.ly/2aUEhWJ

Our Halloween tradition is to carve the plastic/rubber pumpkins one can buy at the craft store. We still do our traditional fresh pumpkin carving with our extended family, but we also do this so that every year we have 'memory' pumpkin. I suggest using the ones that say 'carve able' and buy the little battery operated carving tool, which will prevent you from hand cramps. We've also used a dremmel tool, but prefer the other so that our son can participate with majority of the carving. In the fall I just turn them around to the non-carved side, and I get my pumpkin patch!

The Wimp Family | Texas

BACK TO SCHOOL SUNDAES

I have always loved back-to-school time. It might have a little something to do with the fact that the first inklings of fall are on the horizon, including crisper mornings, apple-picking on the calendar, and maybe even slight yellowing of leaves. As a child, I would be so excited to choose my first-day-of-school outfit, see who my new teacher was going to be, and to get brand new school supplies. I am still thrilled by brand new pencils and paper, and going down the school supplies aisle at the store I'm tempted to buy one of everything just for me!

A fun way to mark the beginning of the school year is with Back-to-School Sundaes the night before school starts. I will actually use any excuse for an ice cream sundae, and this is a great one! I make a mean homemade hot fudge, and a caramel sauce that just can't be beat. Add in other toppings like whipped cream, maraschino cherries, and chopped nuts, and it's really a party!

We set up a sundae bar, and let everyone go through to choose the toppings they want—creating their very own ice cream masterpiece. I'm a caramel girl, so that's always my first priority!

Sitting down and eating our sundaes together is a great time to talk about the upcoming year—what they're excited for, nervous about—or just to listen to them chatter about teachers and friends and even riding the school bus, which is what my twin boys can't wait for this year as they start kindergarten. Giving them a platform to express themselves is even more important than the ice cream, but combining the two is a wonderful way to do it.

While we're eating our sundaes, we also decide on a personal goal to go along with each topping. It can involve friends, academics, and personal characteristics. Doing better in math, having the courage to make new friends, standing up for what they believe in even when it's hard—these are all examples of some of the goals that might be set. My husband and I aren't exempt from the goal-setting, as we both have things we want to work on. The beginning of a calendar year is known for its resolutions, but we feel the same about a school year. It's the perfect time to think about what we want to learn, things we want to experience, and ways we can grow. And the ice cream is pretty good too.

· · · · · ·

CARAMEL PECAN SAUCE
INGREDIENTS

1½ cups chopped pecans

7 Tbsp. butter (divided)

1½ cups brown sugar

3 Tbsp. flour

¾ cups light corn syrup

⅔ cups evaporated milk

- Place the pecans in a microwaveable dish (I use a glass pie plate) with 3 Tbsp. butter.

- Cook for 7–9 minutes, stirring twice. Watch them VERY carefully so they don't burn!

- In another microwave safe bowl (I like using glass bowls—a glass batter bowl is my favorite), place remaining butter and heat until melted. Whisk in brown sugar, flour, corn syrup, and evaporated milk until blended. Cook on high 6–8 minutes, stirring 2–3 times, until the sugar is dissolved.

- Add in the pecans, and stir well. Pour into jars! Makes approximately 3 cups of sauce.

TIP: If you're looking forward to the holidays, Caramel Pecan Sauce also makes wonderful holiday and neighbor gifts. Pour it in mason jars, and tie a cute ribbon and tag around the lid.

BREAKFAST WITH DAD

One of the most anticipated traditions begins with the start of each school year!

Once a week, one of the kids gets a turn going with their dad to breakfast. They get to go before school to the cutest breakfast place down the road, order fluffy pancakes, and drink hot chocolate smothered with whipped cream. My daughter gets to go to a gluten-free bakery and have an enormous cupcake . . . for breakfast! We want it to be extra special in every way, so our normal "what's for breakfast" rules go out the window . . . just for the day.

It's the perfect time for conversation—for them to have time with their dad, laughing, talking, and having fun. After breakfast they get a ride to school in dad's car, which is the proverbial icing on the cake. It's a morning that they eagerly look forward to, and one that all parties enjoy thoroughly! We have six children, and with my husband's work schedule, it can take a couple of months for everyone to have their turn. Then we start over again, and repeat throughout the entire school year.

We've always felt very strongly about giving our children one-on-one time with each parent—where the distractions of home and life can't come into play, and where some real connecting can happen. It's a time to share good things, happy things, sad things, hard things, and things that might only be uttered in the quiet confines of a breakfast for two. We had one child for many years, and even though he was always the only one at home, and got a lot of individual attention, we still had regular date nights and outings with him. As our family has grown, we've gotten more creative on how to accomplish that with each child, and "Breakfast with Dad" is something that's been a huge hit.

This is a fun idea for anyone wanting to spend a little extra-special time with kids—moms, dads, grandparents, aunts, uncles, and even older siblings. It can be done last minute, as a surprise, or with a lot of planning, but no matter what, they'll love it, and you'll make some memories!

• • • • • •

FALL BUCKET LIST

I don't think there's a way that I could possibly explain how much I love and adore fall. As much as I enjoy summer, I'm always anxious for those crisp mornings to appear. No matter what the temperature is, when September 1st hits, out comes all of my fall décor, and I'm hoping that those welcoming ways will help it appear even faster. I've lived in both hot and cold climates and either way, I'm ready!

Fall is full of sweaters, pumpkin patches, apple cider, donuts, hayrides, jack-o-lanterns, bonfires, baking, apple orchards, fun holidays, and more time spent with family and friends. It's just *cozy.*

It's also one of the busiest times of the year—with school starting, and all the activities that go with it. Homework, sports, music, dance—there are so many good and important things in our lives, but I know how easy it is to let time go by and realize that you've missed out really enjoying life to its fullest.

I have this distinct memory of going to the grocery store with my then three-year-old son. It was just the two of us, it was autumn, and I had just finished a college class and picked him up from preschool. I remember stacks of apples, pumpkins, gourds, and samples of caramel dip greeting us as we walked in the door, and something just came over me—all of my homework was put aside, all the cleaning and laundry that needed to be done was forgotten for the moment, and we spent the day together, enjoying everything the fall had to offer. For some reason, that day has stayed with me, perhaps as a reminder of what's most important. I don't recall the details of anything else—not the class I was taking, what I was writing my paper on, and not what my house looked like—but I do know that I had a wonderful day with the cutest three-year-old ever! I learned a lesson that day that stayed with me and I'm so grateful for it, especially now that we've added five more children and a lot more onto our calendar.

Enter in our fall bucket list! Often over dinner one night in August, we'll discuss all the things we want to do during the fall and then make our to-do list. It reminds us to make room for family time and to not let the busyness of life take over; to stop and smell the apple cider donuts! We've discovered some of our most favorite family traditions in the fall, and we look forward to them all year.

When we lived in a warm climate, fall didn't look the same as it does now in New York. Even though we didn't have all the fall leaves and crisp weather, there were some traditional fall activities we could do, like going to the pumpkin patch and making pumpkin bread. We also created a our own fall bucket list that included things that we could do because we lived where it was warm, like camping, going to the zoo on Halloween, and visiting the beach. It was our own fall list and we tailored it to our family and where we lived.

· · · · · ·

PRINT YOUR OWN FALL BUCKET LIST

Enter one of the URL addresses below in your computer's address bar and save the file to your computer. You can either print it at home onto white cardstock (the 8x10 size), or you can get it printed at your favorite photo center.

8x10 size:

bit.ly/2b3lLxC

11x14 size:

bit.ly/2b8bs8W

No matter where you live, if you have a leaf-changing fall or not, a fall bucket list is a really great way to not only enjoy the season, but to create some memories as a family, and perhaps establish some new traditions!

happy fall | bucket list

☐ jump in leaf piles ☐ BAKE PIES
☐ visit the pumpkin patch
☐ go on a nature walk ☐ pick apples
☐ GO THROUGH A CORN MAZE
☐ sit by the fire ☐ bake fall cookies
☐ make caramel apples
☐ carve pumpkins ☐ rake leaves
☐ trick-or-treat ☐ DECORATE
☐ tailgate ☐ go on a hayride
☐ roast pumpkin seeds
☐ have s'mores & bonfire ☐ drink apple cider
autumn splendor | sweater weather | Fall
☐ COUNT OUR BLESSINGS

An impromptu tradition that my husband started several years ago was taking our daughters out to buy donuts in their pajamas on Thanksgiving morning. The girls love the novelty of going out in their pj's just with dad to pick their very own donut, and they like that we bend the rules of a "healthy" breakfast to enjoy the tasty treats. Sometimes the best traditions come from a quick idea that catches on and everyone looks forward to each year. I love that it is a special thing that my husband does with his girls.

The Johnson Family, | Texas

THE PUMPKIN PATCH

It all started in St. Johns, Michigan. Our little family of three had just moved there from Utah for graduate school. It was early fall, the leaves were beginning to change colors, and we were enthralled with the gorgeous scenery and our autumn surroundings. A new friend recommended that we drive a short distance to Uncle John's Cider Mill, and so we did—and fell in love.

Our little boy had just turned two, and I don't think he could have loved a place more. With a wooden train and truck, tricycle race car track, corn maze, apple cider and donuts, horse rides (their names were Doc and Dan), and a huge pumpkin patch, it quickly became one of our most beloved fall traditions.

After graduate school we moved a couple hours away and not only did we still love to visit Uncle John's, we discovered more cider mills and pumpkin patches closer to home. Every year we visited these places as a family at least once and I would take the younger kids not yet in school several times throughout the fall.

Our story continued ten years later, with a huge move to Texas; a very different place from Michigan. On the opposite border of the country with a hot and humid climate, I was nervous that we wouldn't be able to continue our fall tradition. Happily, I was wrong.

While it wasn't exactly the same, and there weren't any cider mills, we learned to appreciate a different type of pumpkin patch—and pick them in our flip-flops!

We have finally settled in upstate New York, and we have cider mills and pumpkin patches very similar to the ones we had in Michigan. The crispness in the air, colorful leaves, hot apple cider, cozy sweaters—they're all a part of our pumpkin patch tradition.

Regardless of where we've lived, or what kind of pumpkin patch we've been to, we've done it the same way. Everyone gets to choose a pumpkin, and it's always fun to see what each child chooses. A week or so before Halloween, we either carve them or decorate them. It's another night of fall fun for our family, and we eagerly look forward to it.

After our experiences of living different places, we discovered that while some parts of the tradition might change or adjustments might need to be made, it's really about the fact that we're doing it together. That's what makes it a tradition—the details aren't necessary. So whether we're picking from a pile of pumpkins in 100+ degree weather in Texas, or in a pumpkin patch wearing sweaters in New York, we do it as a family, and that's what matters.

· · · · · ·

TOASTED PUMPKIN SEEDS

I'll admit it. Cleaning out a pumpkin in order to carve it is not my favorite thing. I happily relinquish that job to my dear husband, who doesn't mind getting in up to his elbows with stringy orange pumpkin guts. I, on the other hand, am perfectly content to help carve and serve treats! The big pumpkin-carving payoff for me is not just the adorable pumpkins that will line our front porch, but comes in the form of toasted pumpkin seeds! I remember these from my childhood, and now I love to make them for my own kids.

I always made them the "original" way—with spices and seasonings—but years ago I started experimenting, and now I have an new favorite. Oh my goodness, cinnamon and sugar pumpkin seeds are so yummy! They're crunchy from the crusted cinnamon and sugar and buttery from the melted butter they're rolled in before baking. Baking two kinds of pumpkin seeds means there is something for everyone—both sweet and salty!

Lots of help is needed in the kitchen for these, and kids love to help rinse seeds, spread them out on foil, and pat them dry. It makes it go much faster, and they feel invested in this yummy treat.

You can make as many or as few as you like, and they're perfect for school lunches, serving to guests at a party, or even wrapping up in cute sacks as fun fall gifts!

· · · · · ·

TOASTED CINNAMON & SUGAR PUMPKIN SEEDS

INGREDIENTS

2 cups pumpkin seeds

2–3 Tbsp. butter, melted

cinnamon and sugar

- · Wash seeds well. Boil seeds in a small amount of water in a medium saucepan for 10 minutes.

- · Spread out evenly on aluminum foil and dry well.

- · Toss the dry seeds in the butter, then coat with cinnamon and sugar.

- · Spread out on a cookie sheet that has been sprayed with non-stick cooking spray.

- · Bake at 225 degrees for approximately 1–1.5 hours or until toasted brown.

TOASTED PUMPKIN SEEDS

2 cups pumpkin seeds

1½ tsp. Worcestershire sauce

2 Tbsp. butter, melted

1¼ tsp. seasoning salt (or table salt, if preferred)

- · Follow same directions as above.

APPLE PICKING & DESSERTS

There is just something about rows upon rows of apple trees and the sights and smells of an apple orchard that are absolutely delightful. Picking apples is really the epitome of fall, and it happens to be one of our family's favorite fall activities. We discovered a new orchard last year when we moved to upstate New York and we all fell in love with it.

The kids were very excited about pulling the wagon up and down the rows, trying to decide which types of apples we were going to pick. There were so many to choose from—at least twenty types with a range of colors, everything from a brilliant red to a muted green. It didn't take too long to fill up our paper bags and we eagerly headed to the scale to find out how many

pounds we had picked. Hot apple cider was the pinnacle of the day, and we headed home happy. This tradition is a favorite for lots of reasons, but mostly because we get to be outside, enjoying nature at its finest together, and then eating what we picked!

If there is an apple orchard near you, it's definitely worth going to check it out. If you don't live near an apple farm, take a trip to your nearest farmers' market and choose your apples!

Making apple crisp and dipping apples in caramel are at the top of our to-do list once we get home with our apples; they are both to-die-for good. My kids love apples and caramel for an after school–snack and Apple Crisp is a regular occurrence for our Sunday night treat.

. . . . . .

CARAMEL APPLE DIP

INGREDIENTS

½ cup granulated sugar

¾ cup sugar

½ cup corn syrup

½ cup butter

⅔ cup whipping cream

dash of salt

DIRECTIONS

· Mix all ingredients in a large saucepan and cook over medium heat, stirring constantly, until the mixture comes to a full boil.

· Remove from heat and let cool, then pour it into a jar.

· Refrigerate until ready to serve!

*Makes about 2 ½–3 cups

APPLE CRISP

INGREDIENTS

2 cups flour

2 cups oats

1 tsp. ground cinnamon

½ tsp. ground nutmeg

1½ cups brown sugar

1½ cups butter

2 quarts cored, peeled, and sliced apples

DIRECTIONS

- Preheat your oven to 350 degrees. In a large bowl, combine the flour, oatmeal, cinnamon, nutmeg, and brown sugar. Cut in the butter until the mixture is crumbly.

- Butter a 9 x 13 baking dish, and layer your apples in the dish. Spread the oatmeal mixture on top of the apples evenly.

- Bake for 45–50 minutes, or until apples are tender and topping is lightly browned.

Every year we host Thanksgiving, and we have a special tablecloth we use. Every person that attends Thanksgiving dinner writes on the tablecloth with a fabric marker about what they are thankful for that particular year. It is my greatest blessing each year to iron that tablecloth and read about everyone's gratitude. There are different people each year in attendance, and everyone is invited to share in this tradition. All who come are asked to share and sign and date it. It really helps frame what Thanksgiving is all about. The beauty of this tradition is that the tablecloth can travel wherever Thanksgiving is for your family. Kids who can't write yet can even participate by an adult tracing their hand. Our tablecloth is very full and we all just love reading it every Thanksgiving.

The Dudley Family | New York

THE PERFECT CARAMEL APPLE

We started making caramel apples in the fall even before we had kids, and it's a tradition that's held true ever since. The crispness of the apple paired with chewiness and richness of the caramel equals perfection! Our favorite time to make them is for a family night in September or October, and it's a night looked forward to by every member of the family.

To make sure we're ready to go, I get all the ingredients prepped, ready, and set out, so we can move easily from one step to the next. I don't make the caramel ahead of time, because it's best to dip the apples soon after it's made, but all of the kids like to watch, and sometimes help stir. Their favorite part though, is "decorating" their apple once it's dipped in the caramel—adding all the fun toppings and making it just how they like it.

To make it even more fun, make extra to deliver to friends and neighbors that night! Sometimes I'll have the kids take one to their teacher on the first day of school, since we start in September. Everyone loves a caramel apple!

· · · · · ·

HERE'S HOW TO MAKE THE PERFECT CARAMEL APPLE!

1. Wash your apples well, and let dry completely. I love Granny Smith apples best for caramel apples, because of the tart and sweet contrast, but I also love Gala or Honeycrisp too. Poke a wooden stick in the center of the apple. I use popsicle/craft sticks you can buy at your local craft store. Sometimes I like to use twigs/sticks from our woods instead of the stick—it gives it fun, rustic look.

2. Okay, ready for the best tip ever? *Sand your apple!* I cannot believe the difference this makes. It really works! I use a fine grit sandpaper, and gently rough up the apple—not taking off any of the skin. Doing this removes some of the waxiness, and allows the caramel to stick more easily.

3. Rub the back-side of a cookie sheet with butter. This is where you'll put your apples to cool after they're dipped. I've found that the apples will stick even to parchment paper or wax paper, so I don't use either one.

4. Make your caramel, following the recipe exactly. You really do need to stir constantly, scraping the sides often If you don't have a candy thermometer, I would invest in one—I use mine all the time. I also use the cold water test-dropping some of the caramel into a cup of cold water is an easy way to see which stage your caramel is at.

TIP: Wait a few minutes after making your caramel to dip the apples. I found that waiting really makes a difference—when it's super hot, it has more of a tendency to slide off. You don't need to wait too long—less than 5 minutes.

CARAMEL FOR PERFECT CARAMEL APPLES

· Combine the first three ingredients in a large saucepan.

· When the butter is melted, add the condensed milk. Stirring constantly, cook to 230 degrees (soft ball stage).

· Take off heat, and stir in vanilla. Let it cool for a few minutes before dipping—super hot caramel is more likely to slide off

· Combine the first three ingredients in a large saucepan.

· When the butter is melted, add the condensed milk. Stirring constantly, cook to 230 degrees (soft ball stage).

· Take off heat, and stir in vanilla. Let it cool for a few minutes before dipping—super hot caramel is more likely to slide off

INGREDIENTS

½ cup butter
1 cup light corn syrup
2 cups brown sugar
1 can sweetened
    condensed milk
1 tsp. vanilla
8–10 apples

5. Dip your apples!

6. Once your apples have been dipped in the caramel, it's time to add any additional toppings, like chocolate, nuts, cinnamon and sugar, chopped candy, etc. I melt chocolate chips in the microwave, and then spoon it into a sandwich bag. Push the chocolate into the corner of the bag, then snip a tiny bit off of the corner—an easy piping bag that makes the best drizzles! I place nuts and chopped candy in bowls so that I can easily roll the apples in them.

FAVORITES

· Dipped/drizzled with white chocolate, then in cinnamon and sugar

· Dipped in chocolate, drizzled in peanut butter, then rolled in PB cups

· White chocolate with chocolate drizzles and toffee bits

7. Once you're finished with each apple, place them on your prepared cookie sheet. I let mine sit for about 10 minutes or so (either in the fridge or at room temperature) to harden before I add any other toppings. Leftover caramel can be poured in a buttered dish to be cut and eaten later.

8. Place apples in the refrigerator to firm up—then you're ready to eat and enjoy.

HALLOWEEN BOOK COUNTDOWN

One of my great loves in life is reading books of all kinds. I also love Halloween. Not the scary, ghoulish, gory kind, but the fun costumes, trick or treating, sugar cookies, and pumpkins-on-the-porch kind. To celebrate both of these, I created a Halloween Book Countdown—a really fun way to count down the thirty-one days to Halloween, starting with October 1st.

• • • • • •

I gather thirty-one Halloween books, and then I either wrap them up and number them, or place them in a cute basket or crate. Every day, beginning with October 1st, we choose one of the books to read. My kids love this tradition, and it's the perfect way to help celebrate the fun part of Halloween!

How does it work? I make a list of some of our favorite Halloween books, along with a few others I want to try, then head to the library. I'm working on collecting our own set, but until then, the library is the perfect resource. It usually has all the titles I'm looking for, plus others that are new to us, which I love.

It's a good idea to head to your library right around the first of the month, to make sure you have a good selection. Checkout dates vary from library to library (we've had two, three, and four weeks), but most of them offer renewals, so you could have the books for the entire month. If they don't offer renewals on holiday books, you can always go a couple of times that month to stock up. It's totally worth it!

A Halloween Book Countdown means cozy nights snuggled up together, a good book, and just maybe a cup of hot chocolate.

Perfection.

DETAILS

You can use a tub, crate, basket, or even a space on your bookshelf to keep your books. This method is nice if you want your kids to be able to choose their own book each night. I also like wrapping them up in paper and placing a number on them, for more of a surprise. Honestly, it doesn't have to be anything fancy to be fun—using a basket you already have is perfect too!

DOWNLOAD TAGS

If you want to wrap your books, I've got spooky numbered tags for you! Enter the following URL into your computer's address bar, save to your computer, then print onto white cardstock.

bit.ly/2aGyBmf

FAVORITE HALLOWEEN BOOKS!

There are so many fun Halloween books, and I'm sharing some of our favorites! The targeted age for most of these books is 3–9. If you have older kids, try reading a chapter or two a day out of a Halloween chapter book, and teens might like something by Edgar Allen Poe.

· · · · · · ·

- *Too Many Pumpkins* by Linda White
- *Pumpkin Soup* by Helen Cooper
- *The Biggest Pumpkin Ever* by Steven Kroll
- *Pumpkin Circle: The Story of a Garden* by George Levenson
- *How Many Seeds in a Pumpkin?* by Margaret McNamara
- *Pumpkin, Pumpkin* by Jeanne Titherington
- *In the Haunted House* by Eve Bunting
- *Room on the Broom* by Julia Donaldson
- *The Night Before Halloween* by Natasha Wing
- *Ten Timid Ghosts* by Jennifer O'Connell
- *The Berenstain Bears Trick-or-Treat* by Stan & Jan Berenstain
- *Big Pumpkin* by Erica Silverman
- *The Vanishing Pumpkin* by Toby Johnston and Tomie dePaola
- *Humbug Witch* by Loran Balian
- *Bugs That Go Bump in the Night* by David A. Carter
- *Five Little Pumpkins* by Dan Yaccarino
- *Scary, Scary Halloween* by Eve Bunting & Jan Brett

- *Peek-a-Boooooo!* by Marie Torres Cimarusti and Stephanie Peterson
- *Mrs. McMurphy's Pumpkin* by Rick Walton
- *It's Halloween* by Jack Prelutsky
- *The Thirteen Nights of Halloween* by Rebecca Dickinson
- *Miss Fiona's Stupendous Pumpkin Pies* by Mark Moulton
- *Happy Halloween, Ladybug Girl!* by David Soman and Jackie Davis
- *The Bumpy Little Pumpkin* by Margery Cuyler and Will Hillenbrand
- *Halloween Night* by Arden Druce
- *Haunted Castle on Hallow's Eve (Magic Tree House #30)* by Mary Pope Osborne
- *All Hallow's Eve: The Story of the Halloween Fairy* by Lisa Sferlazza Johnson & Tucker Johnson
- *Pumpkin Hill* by Elizabeth Spurr
- *Skeleton Hiccups* by Margery Cuyler and S.D. Schindler
- *The Ugly Pumpkin* by Dave Horowitz
- *Trick-or-Treat Countdown* by Patricia Hubbard

ANNUAL HALLOWEEN PARTY!

Kim Byers, TheCelebrationShoppe.com

Our little family is big on traditions. We like the idea of preserving our favorite memories by making new ones to add to them year after year. I read somewhere once, if you skip an activity one year it's no longer a tradition. Well, the Byers family is skipping nothing. We may change it up a bit, but letting go entirely is not an option.

One of my fondest childhood memories is a Halloween party my mom planned for me and all my little girlfriends when I was about 10 years old. There were sweets, ghost stories, and a crazy amount of giggles. When my boys were just toddlers I decided I wanted to start those same kind of fun magical memories for them. Being too small to have their own friends just yet, and being too cute in those silly little Halloween costumes not to show them off, I decided to invite all of our neighbors over for a Halloween costume party. We had so many laughs and it was the perfect way to see each other one last time before we all started hibernating. (Here in Ohio, you pretty much run from your car to your house in the winter. There is no meandering around the yard to chat in the bitter wind.) For years, this was the perfect scene.

Then, as my boys grew (and the neighborhood kids grew), there were fewer costumes to see, but more memories to make. So when my boys hit ages ten and eight, we switched out the costumes for pumpkin carving, they started inviting their best friends and it has been a blast! I still get to make all the fun foods, decorate the house like crazy, see all of my friends and theirs, and the boys get to be creative and scrape pumpkin slime. It's a win win!

· · · · · ·

A few tips for hosting a Halloween Pumpkin Carving Party of your own:

- **BYOP Invite**
  Have your guests bring their own pumpkin. This will keep anyone from being disappointed with the one they get to carve.

- **Location**
  I suggest two spots in your home. One that you can decorate with all the fun (indoors) and the second for actual carving (outdoors).

- **Activities Order**
  I suggest starting with all the indoor activities (while their clothes are still pristine and you can get great pictures). These would include crafts, the pumpkin design and treats.

- **Pumpkin Prep**
  When it comes to pumpkin carving, I suggest keeping the pumpkins indoors until you carve. There is nothing worse than cold pumpkin slime. I also suggest tables, disposable cloths, buckets and lots of supplies so the kids can be as creative as they want!

We love this little tradition and I can see it being one that survives until my boys leave for college . . . and then I plan on reinstituting the Halloween costume tradition when I have grandbabies. We'll just keep the cycle going.

HAUNTED GINGERBREAD HOUSES

This year marks our 10th Annual Haunted Gingerbread House Party! We invite friends over to eat, decorate houses, then sit around the campfire and enjoy the crisp fall evening. It's one of our most beloved Halloween traditions and our entire family looks forward to it. Making gingerbread houses at Halloween is just as fun as making them at Christmastime, but spookier!

We send out invites a couple of weeks in advance with a couple of key elements: have everyone bring a milk carton for each child to decorate, plus a couple of bags of Halloween candy. This gives us a greater variety of candy and ensures that we have plenty to go around. For every piece that goes on a house, there's at least one piece that goes in a mouth! I always provide the frosting, graham crackers, and more candy.

We like to have it outside, so I look for a weekend in October with the best weather. If you aren't going to have weather nice enough, setting up tables in the garage is another option. We've lived the majority of our married life in Michigan or New York, so having a back-up plan has always been a part of the party.

· · · · · ·

ITEMS YOU NEED

1. Milk Cartons

If you can get your hands on milk cartons from school, those are the best! If you can't, I like using the pint-sized whipping cream containers. For smaller kids, the half pint size also works well. I've found that the generic brand is best, because they don't have the screw on lid on the side of the carton (which makes it really hard to decorate). Just pour the cream into another container to use later, rinse well, and let dry.

CANDY IDEAS

mini Oreos
Andes mints
Whoppers
Junior Mints
orange slices
black licorice
seasonal M&Ms
(black and orange)
candy corn
peach rings
marshmallows
(the Halloween ones
are cute too!)

2. Candy

For Halloween, I like to focus on black and orange candy to make the houses spooky! For as many kids as we have coming, I have that many different kinds of candy. You'll need something for the candy to be in, and I like to use large black plastic Dixie cups if I'm going informal, and cute see-through containers/bowls if I'm fancy-ing it up. I've done it both ways, and loved it both ways!

3. Candy containers for kids

When it's time to start decorating, the kids will need to go collect candy for their houses, so you need some kind of container for them to use. Clear plastic cups work well, but I've also cut down paper lunch sacks so they're about 4–5 inches tall, and they worked really well too.

4. Plate and Plastic Knife per child

5. Graham Crackers

Buy the cheap ones. They aren't for eating (although they might be eaten!), and so they don't need to be the best tasting. If they have the pint-sized milk containers, it takes a little over one package per house. I also plan on a few extra just in case.

6. Frosting

This is the only time I buy canned frosting! I plan one container for every two children, and I usually have a little leftover.

Ready, set, decorate!

After the houses are decorated, we love to make a whole night of it, with a campfire, badminton, croquet, bocce ball, and more. It's one of the best nights of the year!

YOU'VE BEEN BOO'ED!

It was a dark fall evening. The kids were giggling in the back seat, amidst an intense conversation regarding strategy—who was going to ring the doorbell, where they would hide, when they would run. As the getaway driver, I was instructed to stay far away, but not too far away, to leave the inside lights off, and keep the engine running. Between them, they had all the bases covered, and it was time to go for it. One of the kids had the treats in hand, while the others were close behind. I watched and waited and listened, and what seemed like minutes later, I heard loud pounding feet and gales of suppressed laughter—some more than others. They piled in the truck, and off we went! We just had to go back and see if the treats were gone, so we circled the block, and then went back to the scene. Our hearts were pounding, and we hoped they weren't looking out the window, but our treats were gone! The mission was a success!

One of our most favorite family traditions is to "boo" our neighbors and friends a few weeks before Halloween. We make up two or three plates of yummy treats, print off cute boo signs and instructions, and then sneak out into the night dressed in black clothing (okay... it's usually our pajamas, but we pretend we're totally undercover), and secretly deliver them. We all love it, and we usually talk about our "undercover missions" for weeks to come (especially the close calls!).

It's a really fun tradition that you can also spread throughout your neighborhood, and when you drop off of the treats, you can leave them with the information and invitation to keep it going.

· · · · · ·

HOW DOES IT WORK?

· Make treats or buy Halloween candy and package it up with a cute "you've been boo'ed" tag—two or three or however many you want to do.

· Deliver the treats to a friend or neighbor, place them on the porch, ring the doorbell, and RUN! It's best to do this at night, under the cover of darkness!

· Along with the treats, leave them a "we've been boo'ed" sign to hang up in their window, and the instructions for what to do next.

DETAILS

I have all the printables you need for your own "You've Been Boo'ed" escapade! Enter the following URL links into your computer's address bar, save to your computer, then print onto white cardstock.

Tags
These are for tying onto your treats!

bit.ly/2b89QPJ

Door Sign
This is the sign that the recipients will place in their window on their door, so everyone knows they've already been boo'ed.

bit.ly/2aGz9bx

You've Been Boo'ed Letter
Include this letter with your treats—it gives all the instructions your recipients need to continue the tradition.

bit.ly/2auNKFX

PRETZEL SPIDERS

When my oldest son was in preschool, a friend of mine brought the most darling Pretzel Spiders for the Halloween snack. Were they ever a hit! I decided to make them for my own kids, and they absolutely loved them. That was it—Halloween wouldn't be the same without them!

They are super easy to make, and I love making them for lunch on Halloween Day. You can tuck them in lunches for school-aged kids, and make them for your little ones at home. I love that they're perfectly spooky for kids—a bit of Halloween fun through a fun snack!

If there is a peanut allergy, you can substitute a flavored cream cheese or even chocolate frosting for the peanut butter. One of my girls can't eat gluten, so I also sub out the crackers and pretzels for gluten-free versions.

· · · · · ·

INGREDIENTS

Ritz crackers (2 per spider)

peanut butter (use flavored cream cheese or chocolate frosting in case of allergies)

raisins (2 per spider)

pretzel sticks (6 per spider)

DIRECTIONS

· Spread peanut butter on the bottom of one of the crackers, then place the pretzel sticks in the peanut butter—3 on each side—for the legs. Yes, I do know that spiders have 8 legs, but it's harder to fit that many pretzels on there, so I just stuck with 6.

· Spread peanut butter on the bottom of the second cracker, them place it on top of the pretzels.

· Add two little dots of peanut butter on the top, near the edge, and stick a raisin in the middle of each dot for the eyes.

We love Halloween at our house. We start planning and making our costumes months in advance. The costume-making becomes a major event in our house. We'll often choose a family costume theme, and these costumes are my favorite to make. The kids really get into it, and feel so excited and proud to go out in their costumes on Halloween.

The Hansens | Utah

TIP: These make a darling classroom gift/ treat or preschool or elementary school and teacher gift. Are you going "booing" this year? (See "You've Been Boo'ed" page 27.) These would be super cute to take!

MUMMY OREO POPS

These darling Mummy Oreo Pops are a simple and fun Halloween treat that's perfect for an afternoon activity with little ones home during the day, or on an evening or weekend to include school-aged children and the whole family.

My kids absolutely love to help in the kitchen. Whether it's making dinner, baking cookies, or any other kitchen project, they want to be involved. That's especially the case when it comes to holidays, and a lot of our celebrations revolve around fun things that we can make together.

Every part of the process is fun and kid-friendly—dipping the Oreos in chocolate, making the mummy's "squiggles," and adding the eyes. Before we start, I lay everything out so we're ready to go, and then we go for it. There's always a lot of tasting involved, so I keep extra spoons handy, especially if we're going to be taking them to someone else. They are seriously adorable, not to mention yummy!

· · · · · ·

SUPPLIES

Oreos (Mega Stuf)
white melting chocolate
mini chocolate chips
lollipop sticks

· Slide the lollipop sticks into the middle of the Oreos. I highly suggest the "Mega Stuf" ones, because the center is thicker, and it's easier to slide the sticks into, and the cookies are less likely to break.

· Melt the chocolate according to package directions. I didn't have any official melting chocolate on hand when we made these, so I used white chocolate chips. Just know that they can be thicker when melted than other melting chocolate, so you have to work quickly. I would also suggest melting just a few at a time, melting more as you need it.

· Dip the Oreos into the white chocolate. The melted white chocolate chips were pretty thick, so I used a spoon to help me coat the front and sides of the Oreo. I don't usually do the back, because it's easier to lay back down, plus I like the contrast from front to back. However, if you want to do the whole thing, you certainly can!

· Fill a piping bag with melted white chocolate, and add a small round tip (you can also use a sandwich bag filled with white chocolate and the very tip cut off, or a squeeze bottle with a fine tip), then go back and forth across the Oreo to create the mummy's "bandages". There really is no right way to do this, and my kids really enjoyed this part!

· Add mini chocolate chips for eyes! Refrigerate until set, and then you can package them as desired. You could wrap in a clear bag, tie a cute ribbon, and use as a Halloween party favor. I folded a piece of washi tape (in Halloween colors) around the stick, and left a little "flag" piece off to one side.

HALLOWEEN SOUP

When I think about what's for dinner on Halloween night, I think SOUP! Growing up, it's what my mom served to my siblings and me before we went trick-or-treating, so it was very natural for me to keep the tradition going. Isn't soup just so cozy? I love filling my kids up with something warm before they head off into the (usually chilly) night. Even when we lived in Texas, where it was still pretty hot at Halloween, it was my way of enjoying fall, and the holiday.

The day of Halloween of is usually a very busy one—it's a day of heading to one school and then the next, for Halloween parades, classroom parties, and last minute costume fixes or errands. It's a day that's perfect for throwing soup ingredients in a crockpot or large stew pot, letting it simmer all day, and then serving to a houseful of hungry kids when you're ready. Making a soup that's chock-full of veggies is also one of my favorite mom tricks—preparing them for probably the most candy-filled night of the whole year!

In the spirit of Halloween, I turn my Taco Soup into Halloween Soup! It's full of eye of newt (pinto beans), wart of frog (kidney beans), guts (pumpkin), tears of lizard (diced tomatoes), legs of spider (ground beef), wings of bat (corn), and bumps of toad (spices). It's a spooky concoction that's perfect for Halloween night!

· · · · · · ·

INGREDIENTS

1 lb. ground beef

1 medium onion, chopped

1½ cups frozen corn

1 can pinto beans

1 can kidney beans

1 large can diced tomatoes

1 can diced tomatoes with green chilies

1 package taco seasoning

1 package ranch dressing mix

DIRECTIONS

· Brown the beef and onion in large stewpot (or saucepan if you're planning to do it all in a crock pot). Add the remaining ingredients and simmer for at least 1 hour, or until ready to serve.

· If you use a crockpot, add the browned beef and onion, then add the rest of the ingredients. Cook on low for 6 hours.

· Serve with grated cheese, sour cream, chopped green onions, diced tomatoes, and crushed tortilla chips or tortilla strips—or Jack-o-Lantern Quesadillas! (pg. 43)

Makes 4-6 servings, I double it for our family.

JACK-O-LANTERN QUESADILLAS

INGREDIENTS

butter

cheese

flour or corn tortillas

- Lay out two tortillas for each quesadilla, and on one of the tortillas, cut out a jack-o-lantern face using a paring knife. You can also buy pumpkin face cookie cutters (mine is by Wilton) that also make it really easy, but a knife works too!

- Melt a little butter in a large saucepan (or on a griddle) set to medium high heat. Set the tortilla with no face on the griddle, sprinkle grated cheese on top, then lay the pumpkin face on top!

- When the bottom side is golden brown, flip it over and let the other side cook until it's also golden brown.

My oldest child loved Halloween so much that he even had a Halloween-themed birthday party in May when he turned three. After that, we began having Halloween parties for our kids every October. Some of our favorite activities have been to decorate graham cracker haunted houses, to wrap each other up with toilet paper to look like mummies, and to make mummy pumpkins. Since the kids are growing up, some of the games and crafts have been replaced with "scary" movies. However, a few things never change. We always have mummy dogs made out of Lit'l Smokies, and ghosts made out of Nutter Butters dipped in white chocolate with mini chocolate chip eyes. We also always trick-or-treat around the house at all of the interior doors. The kids especially love when my husband answers one of the doors covered in a sheet like a ghost.

The Danas | San Diego

AUTUMN WASSAIL

My heart beats a little faster when I wake up on an autumn morning and feel a crispness in the air and see the very first leaves on the trees start to yellow and change colors. The thought of pumpkins, cider, sweaters, and cozy evenings around the fire makes me immediately start craving soups, breads, and my all-time favorite Autumn Wassail.

My love for wassail actually started in high school when my AP English teacher hosted her annual wassail event. I fell hard for the warm, spicy, cinnamon-y goodness and I've served it my own home since I was married. It's now a fall staple and I look for every opportunity to make it. It's perfect for holidays, parties, and your own family's enjoyment

This recipe doesn't just taste delicious; it fills your home with the most delightful aroma. Oh my goodness, the smell of it is the epitome of fall. Cinnamon, nutmeg, cloves, orange, pineapple, and apple are combined for the best autumn drink around! Best of all, it's incredibly easy to make and the magic happens all day while it's sitting in your crockpot.

It's a wonderful autumn tradition, and enjoying steaming mugs of Autumn Wassail makes the season just about perfect.

· · · · · · ·

INGREDIENTS

12 cups apple juice
4½ cups pineapple juice
6 Tbsp. lemon juice
2 cinnamon sticks
½ tsp. nutmeg
½ cup brown sugar
2 oranges
24 whole cloves

DIRECTIONS

· Combine first 6 ingredients in crockpot.

· Slice oranges into thick slices and poke 4 cloves into the rind of each slice. Float them on top, then place cover on crockpot.

· Warm through on medium-low heat, then simmer for as long as you like!

THANKSGIVING TREE

I love Thanksgiving for many reasons, but at the top of the list is that it's a time we really focus on the abundance of things we have to be grateful for. It's the perfect time to take even more of an opportunity to talk about those things together as a family—really take a concentrated, daily look of just how much we've been given, how much we have, and how we can show that gratitude.

I've learned that our family does well with visual cues—something we can look at everyday and serve as a reminder of what we're learning. Over the years I've used a variety of different methods to help us count our blessings and document them visually. A few years ago I made a "Thanksgiving Tree" out of wood, and it's become a favorite. Each year I cut leaves out of paper—cardstock and scrapbook paper—and then every day we write something we're grateful for on a leaf and add it to the tree, then talk about it at dinner that night. The very young kids love to color or write (depending on their age), and just get excited about the whole process in general. As they get older, they're able to think in more detail about what gratitude means, and it sparks some really good table discussions.

By Thanksgiving Day, our tree is covered in leaves that represent our life, and give us much-valued visual perspective on what's important. It's the perfect way to start the conversation at Thanksgiving dinner!

· · · · · ·

IDEAS FOR COUNTING YOUR BLESSINGS

· Cut blank strips of paper, then write on them each day and add to a basket or mason jar.

· Write in a family gratitude journal through the month of November. You can keep on going throughout the whole year!

· Cut a tree out of kraft paper (you can get long rolls at any hobby store like Michael's or Hobby Lobby), and adhere it to a wall, door , or even large window. Cut leaves out of colored paper (cardstock and scrapbook paper work well). Write on a leaf each day of November (you can have each person do one every day, or one for the family, whatever you like!), and add them to your tree!

· Find a large frame (8x10 or larger), remove the glass, and paint one side of it with a light colored spray paint or latex paint. Replace the glass, with the unpainted side facing forward. Hang it on a wall, or on a stand. It's now a dry-erase board! You can use a Sharpie (it stays on better than a dry erase marker, but comes off easily with Windex) to write your blessings on the glass. It's super cute, and can be used over and over again!

· A very good friend of mine made this most darling tree and shared it with us years ago. She filled a clay pot with green floral foam, and covered it with moss. She found a branch of a tree that had some smaller branches coming off of it and stuck the base inside the foam. She made leaves out of paper, punched holes in the top, and added loops of jute, so they could be hung on the tree. A cute ribbon around the top of the pot was the perfect touch!

· Make a chalkboard! Find a large frame, remove the glass, and paint one side with chalkboard paint. (I like the spray paint version for this project.) Place the glass back in the frame, with the chalkboard side facing the front. Write "GIVE THANKS" at the top (or use vinyl lettering if you like), and now you've got a fun Thanksgiving chalkboard! It's definitely something you can leave up all year round.

When my kids were young, but old enough to want to play with school friends, we started the tradition "Friday Treats". Every Friday, my kids were allowed to invite any and all the kids they wanted to come over to our house after school. They would play for about an hour and a half and I would provide treats. Some Fridays we would have ten to twelve kids and some Fridays we would have fifty or more! As my kids started getting older, they would sit around the kitchen table eating treats and planning what they would do and where they would go Friday night or Saturday. It was great for me as a mom to know where they were and who they were with. Often times, "Friday Treats" ended up lasting late into the night when my kids were older. It was a great opportunity for me to get to know my kids' friends and welcome them into our home.

The Jameson Family | Arizona

Thirteen years ago, we found ourselves far away from family and friends for Thanksgiving for the first time in our lives. This was difficult for several reasons, but for my husband, missing out on pie was just plain awful. Even though I intended on making him his favorite apple pie, he was disappointed that there would not be a variety of pies to taste. And so, pie night was born. We invited some new friends from church, and other law students. The rule was that you had to bring a pie. That first pie night was epic; there was pumpkin cheesecake, fruit pies, cream pies, and lots of other goodies. Our apartment was packed, and we had a great time. We have continued this tradition every year on Thanksgiving night, everywhere we have lived. There is always someone new. We have watched little kids turn into teenagers. Families have moved in, and moved out. We always try and include those that don't have somewhere to be on Thanksgiving. Sometimes, it is standing room only, especially now that my husband sends out his invitation using social media. The unofficial theme has become, "more pie than people". We have to pull in extra tables, extra chairs, and I have at least a dozen pie servers. We have only added one new rule; if you brought a pie, you must take what's left of the pie home. Otherwise, we end up with more pie leftovers than anyone needs.

The Wirick Family | Utah

CHRISTMAS

A CHRISTMAS COUNTDOWN
EVERYDAY FAMILY CHRISTMAS ACTIVITIES

The best part of Christmas isn't Christmas morning. Don't get me wrong—I absolutely love the magic of Christmas Eve and Christmas morning, and seeing the joy in my children's faces as they tiptoe down the stairs, see the tree lit with all the presents underneath it, peek into their stockings for the first time, and open that one gift that they've been praying for (and that I've been dying to give them). For me, it's everything that leads up to that morning—all the wrapping, shopping, decorating, baking, reading, light-seeing, concerts, plays, parties, craft-making, snuggly movie and popcorn nights, Secret Santa runs, visits with family and friends, sleigh rides in the snow, singing of Christmas songs and caroling with friends, ice skating, reading stories by the fire, and serving others. I love the journey as much as or more than the destination, and I love how it brings out little family closer and establishes much-loved traditions.

One way to coordinate all of these fun Christmas activities is with an advent calendar—a Christmas activity advent with an activity per day from December 1st through Christmas Day. It can be as simple as reading a Christmas book, going for a winter walk, making hot chocolate, or creating paper snowflakes. Other times there may be more prep work needed, like making neighbor treats and delivering them, or a service project. We also love family Christmas outings, and those are on the list too.

Each year I compile a list of activities we want to do, and then schedule them out based on what we have going on and if it's a school day or weekend. Every morning the kids get to see what we're going to do that day, and it's something to look forward to. It's how we celebrate Christmas, and enjoy both new and favorite traditions. When we fill our days with Christmas, it fills our hearts with love for the people in our family, and for those we serve. The Christmas spirit is a real thing, and can bring so much happiness into our homes.

I take our compiled list, type up all of the activities, and print them out onto white cardstock. I cut them into strips, with each activity on its own slip of paper. I've displayed our countdown many different ways, but recently they've been slipped into tiny, numbered paper sacks. Before I place them in the sacks, I look a the calendar, and make sure I'm coordinating easier and more simple activities on busy school days, and the more time-intensive activities on weekends or nights I know we're free. I clip them in order onto a long piece of twine, and it becomes not only a countdown, but also really adorable Christmas décor! Each day we take down a paper sack, and then do the activity that's inside. My kids get so excited to look inside and find out what we're going to do that day! Each activity is like a Christmas present all on its own, and we absolutely love our Christmas Activity Countdown.

· · · · · ·

CHRISTMAS COUNTDOWN DISPLAY IDEAS

· Slip them inside cute envelopes or paper treat bags. Seal with washi tape or tie shut with ribbon. Number them in the order you want them to be.

· Place them inside numbered miniature paper bags. Use tiny clothespins to clip them onto a long piece of twine or ribbon. Hang on a mantel, across a large doorway or opening, or along a banister.

· Adhere them to a 12 x 12 piece of cardstock in the order that you want them to be, and cross one off each day.

· Instead of using the printables, write and number your activities on a large chalkboard. You can also use a large frame by removing the cardboard backing then replacing the glass. Use a fine-tip Sharpie marker (it will come off

with Windex, but won't rub off easily with your hand) to write out your activities on the glass, then cross them off or erase them each day.

· Write the activities onto large craft sticks, and number them on one side. Decorate one end with Christmas washi tape if desired, and place in a mason jar. Choose one stick per day, and turn it upside down when finished.

· Make a numbered paper bunting and adhere the tags to the back.

· Make a paper chain with 25 links, and write an activity on each link.

I've also made an even bigger list of fun Christmas activities as another resource, and they are divided by category, to make it easier to find what you might be looking for.

CHRISTMAS COUNTDOWN ACTIVITIES IDEA LIST

SERVING OTHERS

· Deliver treats to your local fire station

· Secret Santa night—deliver treats secretly to friends and neighbors.

· Serve at a soup kitchen or do other volunteer work.

· Visit a local nursing home—go caroling and visit with the residents.

· Surprise your neighbors and shovel their walks and driveways (especially the elderly, that might have a difficult time).

· Participate in a clothing, food, or toy drive.

· Write notes of appreciation for the people that help you—the bus driver, postal worker, teachers, etc.

· Do the 12 days of Christmas for another family, or someone who needs some holiday cheer.

· Gather gently used toys and then donate them to your local children's hospital.

· Find a giving tree through your church or town that lets you help another family in need. Shop for those gifts together, and then donate them.

· Send a care package to a missionary or family member.

IN THE KITCHEN

· Make homemade hot chocolate—have a hot chocolate bar with lots of toppings.

· Make and decorate sugar cookies.

· Try a new Christmas recipe.

· Have snowman pancakes for dinner.

· Have a baking day—make all of your favorite cookies and candy.

· Make hot apple cider.

· Make homemade donuts when it snows for the first time.

· Make treats for friends and neighbors.

· Make a holiday meal from another country or culture.

· Cut sandwiches with Christmas cookie cutters for your kids' lunches.

· Make caramel popcorn.

CRAFTS/DECORATIONS

· Make handmade ornaments.

· Make paper snowflakes and decorate the windows.

· If you don't have snow, make a snowman out of paper.

- Make reindeer food for Christmas Eve: oats and a little glitter.
- Make homemade gifts for each other.
- String popcorn and cranberry garland.
- Decorate paper wreaths and hang them on bedroom doors.
- Make homemade Christmas cards.

FUN AT HOME

- Have a Christmas movie marathon.
- Watch a Christmas movie and eat popcorn.
- Have a campout under the tree one night.
- Put on a Christmas play.
- Have a fancy dinner one night, and get all dressed up.
- Have a red and green dinner.
- Create a holiday playlist of all your favorite Christmas songs.
- Look at pictures from Christmases past.
- Snuggle up and read a Christmas book every night until Christmas Day
- Build a snowman.
- Have a snowball fight.
- Write letters to Santa and mail them.
- Make and decorate gingerbread houses.
- Roast marshmallows in the fireplace or over the stove.
- Put on a Christmas play.
- Have a family game night.
- Stuff and stamp Christmas cards.
- Act out the Nativity.
- Put up Christmas lights outside.
- Watch funny Christmas videos on YouTube.
- Celebrate St. Nicholas Day on December 6th by doing a secret act of kindness.
- Leave candy in your kids' shoes to celebrate St. Nicholas Day.
- Track Santa at **www.noradsanta.org** (starting December 1st)

- Invite friends over for a Christmas sing-along.
- Have a cookie exchange party.
- Have an ugly sweater party.
- Pile in mom and dad's bed for a Christmas movie.
- Facetime or Skype family and friends that live far away.

FAMILY OUTINGS

- Go ice skating.
- Go for a sleigh ride.
- Cut down or pick out your Christmas tree.
- Pile in the car in your jammies and drive around to see Christmas lights.
- Go for a late night hot chocolate run.
- Attend a Christmas concert or performance, like The Nutcracker.
- Go to the library and check out Christmas books.
- Bundle up and go for a winter walk.
- Visit Santa.
- Pick out new ornaments for your tree
- Go Christmas shopping together.
- Deliver neighbor treats and gifts.
- Gather friends and go Christmas caroling
- Attend a Christmas parade.

CHRISTMAS MOVIES

- Little Women
- Meet Me in St. Louis
- Elf
- Miracle on 34th Street (definitely the original, in color)
- It's a Wonderful Life
- White Christmas
- The Polar Express
- A Christmas Carol (Jim Carrey version)
- Mickey's Christmas Carol

- One Magic Christmas
- Babes in Toyland
- Holiday Inn
- How the Grinch Stole Christmas (cartoon version)
- Rudolph the Red-Nosed Reindeer

- Frosty the Snowman
- Holiday Affair (1940's)
- Truce in the Forest
- The Nativity Story
- Charlie Brown's Christmas

· · · · · · · · · · ·

You want to try adding in a few new Christmas traditions . . . where do you start?

EXPLORE YOUR TOWN & AREA

One of the biggest resources for really fun family Christmas activities is the place where you live—many of the things we love to do during the holidays are local events or places that have become a part of our celebration. Every time we move someplace new, I always ask around for others' favorite places to go and things to do. I'll ask anyone—a hair stylist, cashier at the grocery store, new friends I made at church or school, neighbors—and soon I've got a list to go from. Most local libraries and cities have their own Christmas activities, concerts, festivals, and even parades to celebrate the holidays, and many of them are free or at low cost. Museums, zoos, and churches are also great places to check.

LEARN FROM OTHERS

Over the years I've gleaned a lot of information from friends and others around me. I love learning about new ideas, and seeing what other families do. I've taken some of those and incorporated them into our family, and it's how many of our traditions were born.

WHAT ARE YOUR FAMILY'S INTERESTS?

The beauty of a Christmas countdown is that no two are alike—because no two families are alike! Think about what you like to do, or what you'd like to try. Do you love outdoor activities? Add ice skating to your list. Do you want to focus completely on service? You can do that. Do you have family members that are homebound? There are plenty of activities you can do without leaving your house! Is your goal to try new things? A Christmas Countdown is the perfect time to do that too. Your list will be about your family, which is what makes it so wonderful!

CHRISTMAS KINDNESS CHAIN

Last year my baby was very ill, and she was hospitalized six times within a ten-month period. She spent two weeks in the PICU of our nearest children's hospital during one admission—intubated and fighting to get better, which she thankfully did. How grateful I was for the amazing nurses, doctors, and volunteers who made our very difficult time in the hospital as comfortable as possible. While I was there, I noticed that they were short of books and toys. With Christmas just about six weeks away, our family knew exactly what we wanted to do. We collected toys and books from friends and people in our community, bought a few new ones, and then took them as a family to donate them to the PICU. It was such an emotional night, but our hearts were full of gladness and thankfulness. It's still one of our most treasured memories, and even though my children were almost all small, they remember too, and the feelings they had.

Acts of service and kindness epitomizes what the Christmas season is truly about, and the feeling you get when serving is a blessing to both the giver and receiver. Our family loves and enjoys all the parts of Christmas—so many fun things to do and see—but focusing on what really matters is the best gift I can give my children and family. When you give of yourself, you're never really the same—it changes how you approach Christmas, and it gives you memories you will cherish for years to come.

A Christmas Kindness Chain is a simple and meaningful tradition—a way to visually see all the acts of service of kindness that our family has given over the Christmas season, and our own gift to Jesus Christ, who is the reason for our celebration.

Instead of creating a chain and taking one off each day, I like to add the chains as we go along, so by the time Christmas arrives, we have a full chain representing all of our acts of kindness. It's the perfect visual reminder for the whole month, and then on Christmas Day we can read through them and remember.

I love doing a construction paper chain because it is so simple, and it's easy for my kids to be a part of. I cut red and green construction paper into 1.5-inch strips (11 inches long), and then write on the strips some of the service ideas we want to do over the next month. They include bigger projects, like participating in a clothing drive, but also things that the kids can do on their own—like smiling at everyone all day, letting someone in front of them in line, opening doors, etc. I also leave some of the strips blank, because I want the kids (and all of us) to look for ways to serve, and then be able to write them down and add them to the chain.

Serving together brings families closer together, and it will be a Christmas you won't soon forget!

At Christmastime, my family does "Warm Fuzzies". Each night before bed we gather around the tree and talk about what we did during the day. We talk about a service that someone did for us, and, more important, what service we did for someone else. The good deeds can be as simple as smiling at a stranger or as big as shoveling snow off a neighbor's driveway. For every service we mention we put a "warm fuzzy" (a large pompom) in a container. Our goal is to fill the jar by Christmas.

Andersen Family | Idaho

donate to

using home

send a package to someone in th

Pay for the person b

leave

Let someone go in fro

shovel someone's drivev

make a meal for someone

Do a chore for

SERVICE IDEAS FOR FAMILIES

- Take treats to the police station and/or fire station
- Shovel someone's driveway
- Put Christmas lights up for someone who isn't able to
- Send a care package to a missionary or someone serving in the military
- Send phone cards to someone in the military so they can call home
- Go through your pantry and cupboards and take canned goods to a food bank
- Donate new or gently used warm hats and gloves to a homeless shelter
- Donate to a giving tree
- Gather toys and books and donate to a children's hospital
- Serve a meal at a local soup kitchen
- Make blessing kits and hand them out to the homeless
- Visit a nursing home and talk to the residents and sing Christmas carols
- Pay for the person behind you in the drive-thru
- Leave candy canes on windshields in the parking lot
- Leave microwave popcorn at a Redbox
- Leave dollar bills in the Dollar Spot at Target with a little note
- Donate pet food to the local pet shelter
- Leave a homemade bookmark in your library book
- Gather blankets and donate to a homeless shelter
- Collect toys and books to donate to a women and children's shelter
- Volunteer at a food bank
- Deliver a Christmas tree and ornaments to a family in need
- Be Secret Santa to a family in need
- Offer to babysit for a young mother or single mom so she can go shopping

- Clean up a park or other area in your town
- Donate a bunch of school supplies to your child's classroom
- Take baby supplies to a women's and children's shelter
- Put together necessity kits for parents who have children in the hospital ICU
- Donate some of the clothes your kids have outgrown to the school nurse
- Bring hot chocolate to the Salvation Army collectors
- Take dinner to another family
- Leave an extra big tip for your waiter
- Right after it snows, go through a parking lot and clean off windshields
- Go Christmas caroling in your neighborhood—bring friends along!
- Leave change in a vending machine
- Put quarters in parking meters

SERVICE IDEAS FOR KIDS

- Do a chore for a sibling
- Smile all day to everyone you see
- Give sincere compliments to those you talk to
- Let someone go before you in line
- Clean your room without being asked
- Make cards for your bus driver and teachers
- Look for someone at school that needs a friend, and go talk to them
- Hold open doors for everyone
- Cover pinecones in birdseed and peanut butter and put them in your backyard
- Go through your toys and choose a few to donate
- Help mom or dad with dinner
- Read to a younger sibling
- Donate your week's allowance or ask your mom and dad how you can earn money, so you can help someone in need.

CHRISTMAS BOOK ADVENT

There is just something so magical about listening to and reading Christmas stories, and it's one of our family's most favorite things to do at Christmastime. It's a perfect way to celebrate the season, and spend some really wonderful time together. What could be more cozy than curling up on the couch each night, snuggling in blankets, and reading about the most beloved time of year?

Every year, I wrap twenty-five Christmas books, usually with brown paper and red twine, with numbers on each one. They include books that are well worn and beloved, and others that we are just discovering. Every day day in December, from the 1st through Christmas Day, my kids open a book for us to read together. Once they're unwrapped, I leave them out so they can continue to read and re-read them—and they do! My little ones at home with me during the day are constantly looking at them, or we are reading them together. When my school kids get home and finish with their homework, they head straight for the Christmas books. Our weekends, and especially Sundays are filled with reading Christmas stories, and it's been a blessing in our home. It's one of our most beloved Christmas traditions, and I love that we end each day with a story that leaves us feeling uplifted and full of the Christmas spirit.

To put this advent together, I am slowly gathering Christmas books. Every year I add to our collection and choose a few more favorites or select a new book to try. To make up the remaining books, I supplement with books from the public library, and in the beginning, before I had very many of our own, I exclusively borrowed from the library. It's a wonderful resource, and I love utilizing all it has to offer.

It's never too early or too late to start your own collection! Just buy one or two favorites a year, or more if you can! Supplementing with library books is the way to go . . . .just be sure to check with them to see how long you can have books out, and plan accordingly. Some libraries allow 30-day checkout periods, and others are 2-3 weeks. If you have children in school, make sure to check their Scholastic book orders—it's a great place to get books at low prices. If you can't buy books now, get all of them from the library, or even try garage sales or thrift shops where you might find a few treasures for cheap.

My children are little, and I choose books accordingly, but I also challenge them a little bit, and select old-time classics and favorites that might be more than their typical listening level. These stories capture their attention, and they feel that extra something special that surrounds them, and they love to listen to even longer books than they might normally. I also include some board books, which my smallest ones love, and are appropriate for babies up to preschoolers. My school kids can be involved by reading these to their siblings, and they love that. I tend to shy away from character books, but if your children love those most, why not add a few to your own library! For those of you with older children, or only adults in the home, try reading a chapter book aloud each night- like our family favorite, *A Christmas Carol*, by Charles Dickens. That's something else we look forward to, and even the little ones listen in.

There are so many wonderful Christmas books, and I'd like to share a list of our family's favorites, in case you're looking for ideas, or a place to start.

· · · · · ·

OUR FAVORITE CHILDREN'S CHRISTMAS BOOKS

1. *Room for a Little One: A Christmas Tale* by Martin Waddell
2. *The Tale of Three Trees* by Angela Elwell Hunt
3. *The Christmas Miracle of Jonathan Toomey* by Susan Wojciechowski
4. *The Christmas Candle* by Richard Paul Evans
5. *The Little Match Girl* by Hans Christian Andersen
6. *The Legend of the Christmas Tree* by Rick Osborne
7. *The Gift of the Magi* by O.Henry
8. *The Year of the Perfect Christmas Tree* by Gloria Houston
9. *Christmas in the Big Woods* by Laura Ingalls Wilder
10. *Who is Coming to Our House?* (Board Book) by Joseph Slate
11. *A Wish to Be a Christmas Tree* by Colleen Monroe
12. *The Polar Express* by Chris Van Allsburg
13. *Mr. Willowby's Christmas Tree* by Robert Barry
14. *Why Christmas Trees Aren't Perfect* by Richard Schneider
15. *Christmas Day in the Morning* by Pearl S. Buck
16. *Winter's Gift* by Jane Monroe Donovan
17. *A Christmas Carol* (picture book edition) by Charles Dickens
18. *The Little Fir Tree* by Margaret Wise Brown
19. *Humphrey's First Christmas* by Carol Hever
20. *Christmas Oranges* by Linda Bethers
21. *Jingle Bells* by Iza Trapani
22. *The Light of Christmas* by Richard Paul Evans
23. *Drummer Boy* by Loren Long
24. *The Nutcracker* by Susan Jeffers
25. *This is the Stable* by Cynthia Cotton

PRINTABLE NUMBER TAGS

I've created number printables to place on top of your wrapped books, so you can put them in order of how you'd like them to be opened. I love using brown paper, red bakers twine, and these adorable numbers!

DOWNLOAD

Enter the following URL in your computer's address bar, and download the file. Print onto white or cream cardstock, or even brown kraft paper. You can either punch a hole in the top of the number, and string it on with twine or ribbon, or tape it on using double stick tape or even cute washi tape!

bit.ly/2b9aUBp

CUTTING DOWN OUR CHRISTMAS TREE

For fourteen years now, we've been cutting down our Christmas tree. It is one of our most beloved and favorite traditions . . . ever. To us it's not hard work, or a lot of effort—it's just one of the things that makes Christmas so special for our family, and it's FUN! There's just something about bundling up and tromping through the snow to cut down your own tree that's just unbeatable. Even on the years we've had no snow, it's just as magical, and we eagerly look forward to it every year.

I grew up with a real tree every Christmas, and it's just one of those traditions that I knew I wanted to carry on with my own family. It's not only the smell of the fragrant pine needles that permeate the whole house, or the charming tree imperfections—it's the wonderful activity of cutting it down, of going out as a family and deciding together which one is the perfect tree for our family. It's just . . . Christmas.

We go the day after Thanksgiving, and we usually have to bundle up—even if there isn't snow on the ground, it's cold enough to warrant coats and snow pants. The two years we lived in Texas we got to wear flip-flops to cut down our tree!

When we get to the tree farm, sometimes we take a hayride out to where the trees are, and other times, when there's snow on the ground, we take sleds. We aren't in a hurry, because the whole process is to be savored. This day only comes once a year! We all walk around and pick our favorite, and then after walking back and forth, and then back again, carefully examining them, we finally select "the one." My husband and oldest son take over the cutting of the tree, but only after we stop and take a picture first, of our family in front of our tree. I have loved looking at those pictures over the years, and seeing how our family has grown and changed.

After our tree is down, it's back on the hay wagon we go! It's hard not to be engulfed in the Christmas spirit out there in the crisp air, surrounded by Christmas trees, as well as other families on their own Christmas tree quest.

Once the tree is baled, it's time to wrestle it on top of our vehicle, and then as we drive away, Christmas songs fill the air and our hearts. The day wouldn't be complete without hot chocolate, and lots of talk of Christmas wishes and plans. It really is the perfect day.

· · · · · ·

DETAILS

- If you're looking for a Christmas tree farm, ask friends and neighbors for their recommendations. You can also search online for tree farms in your area. Read about what kind of trees they have, and what you need to bring with you.
- Asking the people at the tree farm about how to best take care of your tree is always a good idea, especially if it's your first time, or if you're selecting a different tree variety than you have in the past. I would also suggest asking before you go out hunting for a tree about what kinds of trees shed more or less needles, have a specific type of smell, or any other items you have in mind.
- Many tree farms also carry fresh garland and wreaths, and I love using them to decorate my door and mantel.
- Make sure you bring what you need to tie the tree onto the top of your vehicle. You can use rope, or even bungee cords, which is what we like.
- You'll need to have a tree stand, so you can put it up when you get home. You can find them at stores like The Home Depot, Lowe's, and your local hardware store.
- You can be outside for awhile, so if you live in a cold climate, bundling up is a good idea!

SUGAR COOKIES & DECORATING THE TREE

I don't remember how these two traditions became intertwined, although I'm not surprised they did. Don't they just seem like they go together—decorating cookies and decorating a tree? We started combining the two many years ago, and after the first year, our kids reminded us that's "what we do." So we did.

It's part two of our tree adventure—with part one cutting down our tree the day before. The day we cut the tree down, we usually try to get it centered and stable in the tree stand (which is usually an adventure in and of itself) and the lights on, so we're ready to go the next day. With lots of little kids at our house, when it's time to decorate the tree, it's best to be ready to go right away!

Most of our decorations are handmade, and many of them have the kids' names, initials, or numbers on them for organizing purposes. They get so excited about being able to put "their ornaments" on the tree, and finding the perfect spot for them to go. They have also helped to make some of the ornaments, and they love reminiscing about how we made them—and some of the funny stories that might accompany them. The star at the top is a bit tricky, because everyone wants to put it on, but we've been known to take it off and on a couple of times so a turn is to be had by each child.

Once the tree is decorated, we're ready for sugar cookies! I make the dough ahead of time, and have it ready for rolling out. We don't roll out all of the dough—about half of it I make into regular round cookies. Maybe one day we'll roll out more, but right now, with so many little helpers, it takes awhile just to do that half of the batch! I've collected plenty of cookie cutters over the years, and they each get to choose the one or two they want to cut out. After they're baked, frosting and sprinkles are ready to be added in abundance (the frosting is the best part, though), and I love watching their individual personalities come through in their decorating techniques and styles.

Their excitement is addicting, and right there in that moment, I close my eyes, and soak it all in. Yes, it's craziness—the flour, dough, frosting and sprinkles that cover them, me, and the entire kitchen—but that laughter, those smiles are worth every minute it takes to clean it all up.

At the end of the day, we have a tree covered in lights and decorations, tummies full of cookies and hot chocolate, and a whole new chapter of memories.

· · · · · ·

HANDMADE CINNAMON ORNAMENTS

I made these cinnamon ornaments for our first Christmas tree when we were first married—very young, and very poor students—and they have been a part of our Christmas tree ever since. There is something just so cozy about making handmade ornaments, in all their lovely imperfection. Perhaps it's the old-fashioned girl in me that wishes I could sit in a log cabin, string a popcorn garland, and hang these cinnamon ornaments on the tree I cut down in the woods. This is my way of capturing a piece of that, and I love it!

The cinnamon ornaments last quite awhile, but every couple of years it's time to make a new batch. It's the perfect activity to do with my kids, and it's become a tradition to make them together. They help with the measuring, stirring, rolling and cutting, and making sure the oven light was on so they could monitor their progress while they were baking. Once they are cool, they help string the twine and brush off remaining crumbs. We have to repeat over and over again that these are NOT to eat, and I think they've finally got it!

One of the most wonderful things about making these ornaments is that they fill your home with the pungent and delightful aroma of cinnamon, and that will continue once they're hung on your tree.

It's super easy to do, and if you're looking for an inexpensive way to trim your tree, this is a great option. The only two ingredients are applesauce and cinnamon, and for less than $5, you should be able to get at least 14 ornaments out of one batch. (That's how many we are usually able to make—using small to medium cookie cutters.) As a final touch, I love to tie my favorite red bakers twine on some, and ribbon on others.

You'll see that our stars are not perfect, but they are perfect for our tree! In this case, their charm comes from their imperfection, and the fact that we made them ourselves. Year after year, these darling ornaments are hung on our tree, and the memories formed while we made them are remembered!

· · · · · ·

CINNAMON ORNAMENTS RECIPE

INGREDIENTS

¾–1 cup applesauce

1 cup + 2 Tbsp. cinnamon (that's how much is in a 4.12 oz. container of McCormick® Ground Cinnamon, if that's easier to buy and use!)

SUPPLIES

cookie cutters

drinking straw

ribbon or twine

DIRECTIONS

WARNING: DO NOT EAT! FOR DECORATION ONLY!

· Preheat oven to 200°F. Mix applesauce and cinnamon in small bowl until a smooth ball of dough is formed. (You may need use your hands to incorporate all of the cinnamon.) Start with ¾ cup applesauce, and then add more if necessary. I ended up adding a little more applesauce—mine was still a little crumbly.

· Using about 1/4 of the dough at a time, roll dough to 1/4-inch to 1/3-inch thickness between two sheets of plastic wrap. Peel off top sheet of plastic wrap. Cut dough into desired shapes with 2 to 3-inch cookie cutters. Make a hole at top of ornament with drinking straw. Place ornaments on a baking sheet covered with parchment paper.

· Bake 2 ½ hours. Cool ornaments on wire rack. To dry ornaments at room temperature, carefully place them on wire rack, and let them stand 1 to 2 days until thoroughly dry.

· Insert ribbon (I used bakers twine!) through holes and tie to hang on your tree!

CHRISTMAS PAJAMAS, POPCORN & A MOVIE

New pajamas and Christmas go together like peanut butter and jelly, and we started giving our kids new pajamas on Christmas Eve when they were tiny. It's a tradition that has held strong, and while some of the details have changed, it's remained as a Christmas tradition staple.

We moved from our home state when we left for graduate school, and we've never lived close since then. Our home has always been thousands of miles away from our families, and we've not always been able to be there for as many holidays and Christmases as we would have liked.

A few years ago, as part of their Christmas presents to the kids, my mom and dad took over giving them their pajamas. It's so fun to have that connection with them, and every time they wear them, it reminds us of their grandparents. It's a special part of the holiday season, and Christmas pajamas are much loved!

For years we opened the pajamas on Christmas Eve, but I was always a little sad that we weren't able to enjoy them for the entire holiday season, and so we came up with a new plan that we all absolutely love. Now we open them on the day we decorate our Christmas tree, and it's perfect! I wrap up the pajamas in one big box, along with microwave popcorn for everyone, and a new Christmas movie or two. It's a whole Christmas night in a box!

It's become just one fun-filled day of Christmas—decorating the tree, sugar cookies, opening up pajamas, and then ending the day with popcorn and a movie. It's such a delightful beginning of the Christmas season, and they can also enjoy their pajamas the entire month! They still wear them on Christmas Eve . . . and as many times as possible before that!

· · · · · ·

HOMEMADE HOT CHOCOLATE

I grew up with and fell in love with hot chocolate being homemade, so that's what I do too. I love when I do things the way my mom did, because it brings back so many memories of my own childhood.

Homemade hot chocolate is a staple during the winter months at our house. We have it after all of our winter activities, like playing in the snow, making snowmen, tubing, and cross country skiing. We even drink it after school on super cold days, on weekends sitting by the fire, and when we have friends over.

It's also a part of all of our holiday moments, including decorating the tree, writing letters to Santa, and watching holiday movies. To be honest, we don't really need an excuse!

It takes just minutes to make, and totally worth it. You can serve it with marshmallows, but we also love it with whipped cream and cinnamon and sugar, or peppermint cream. We also like to experiment with different flavors, and a couple of our favorites are Mexican Hot Chocolate and Toasted Coconut Hot Chocolate. But no matter how you make it, it's always creamy and delicious!

· · · · · · ·

HOT CHOCOLATE

INGREDIENTS

1½ cups milk chocolate chips

1 can of evaporated milk

3–4 cups whole milk

1 tsp. vanilla

DIRECTIONS

· In a saucepan over low heat, melt the chocolate chips with the can of evaporated milk. Once they're melted, stir in milk (amount varies depending on how chocolate-y you want it) and heat through.

· Remove from heat and add the vanilla. Serve with Peppermint Cream!

MEXICAN HOT CHOCOLATE

1½ cups milk chocolate chips

1 can evaporated milk

3–4 cups whole milk

1 tsp. vanilla

1–2 tsp. ground cinnamon

¼ tsp. nutmeg

· In a large saucepan over medium heat, melt the chocolate chips with the evaporated milk.

· Once they're melted, stir in the whole milk, then add the cinnamon, nutmeg, and vanilla. Start with 1 teaspoon of cinnamon, and add more if desired. Heat through, then serve with whipped cream, chocolate shavings, and a sprinkle of cinnamon.

PEPPERMINT CREAM

INGREDIENTS

1 pint heavy cream

¼ cup powdered sugar

1 tsp. peppermint extract

2 candy canes, crushed

DIRECTIONS

· In a mixing bowl, beat the heavy cream until it's just beginning to form soft peaks.

· Add the powdered sugar (you can do more or less to taste), and beat until incorporated. Add the peppermint extract and crushed candy canes, then beat again until the right consistency.

· I like to spoon the cream into a sandwich bag, push it down into one corner, snip the corner off of the bag, and then pipe it onto the top of the hot chocolate. Sprinkle a few more bits of candy cane on top, and enjoy!

TOASTED COCONUT HOT CHOCOLATE

INGREDIENTS

one 12 oz. bag chocolate chips

1 can coconut milk

4–5 cups milk

sweetened coconut

chocolate shavings (from a chocolate bar)

whipping cream

DIRECTIONS

· Melt the coconut milk and chocolate chips in a large saucepan over medium heat, stirring pretty regularly. When the chips are melted, slowly add the regular milk. Start with 4 cups, and add more to taste, and depending on if you like it a little bit thicker, or on the thinner side. Heat through.

· In a large skillet, toast the sweetened coconut over medium heat—stir constantly with a wooden spoon until they become golden brown. It doesn't take long!

· To serve, top the hot chocolate with whipped cream, toasted coconut, and chocolate shavings.

A NIGHT OF CHRISTMAS LIGHTS

It's forever imprinted in my mind . . . the little voice of my two year-old little boy, squealing, "wites, wites, oh, the wites", over and over again. Translation? He was talking about the Christmas lights we were looking at, and he was absolutely beside himself with joy. It was so simple—just a ride through our neighborhood one Sunday evening, but it was his absolute favorite Christmas activity of the whole season. I wish I could have bottled it up to save and listen to from year to year, because just the thought of it makes me smile.

In the town where we live, there is one house not far from us that goes above and beyond. They have all of their lights coordinated with music to create an absolutely incredible light show. There's a radio station that you tune to, so the music streams into your car, while you sit and watch the lights dance and flicker to the beat of each song. My kids—the same ones that can't still for ten minutes doing anything else—sit and watch in pure rapture. It's usually an hour before we can even consider leaving!

There's just something about a house all lit up with Christmas lights, and I love how it makes the whole street brighter, happier, and more joyful. They are an outward representation of the Christmas spirit that fills us, and we usually go out driving to see them more than once or twice during the holiday season. We love Christmas lights so much that it's on my list to ask friends and neighbors about when we move to a new place.

Our night of Christmas lights means getting cozy in our pajamas, bringing along bags of popcorn to munch on, and turning up the Christmas music! It's when we're at our silliest, and we can talk about the most things. I just love being in the car together. We can turn the music up loud, make up silly new words to the Christmas songs, and just be together with no other distractions. It's so incredibly simple and costs no money, but odds are, it will be one of the best nights of the year!

· · · · · ·

Go on a Christmas Lights Scavenger Hunt! I created a fun checklist with pictures and words, so it works for both the younger and older children and teenagers. You can even get together with other families to make it a competition, and see how many items you can each cross off within a certain time limit. My kids absolutely love each having their own list, and scanning the houses and yards for something to check off.

To download the printable checklists, copy and paste the following links into the address bar of your browser. Open up the files, save to your computer, and print!

Scavenger Hunt With Pictures:

bit.ly/2b1s3wE

Scavenger Hunt Without Pictures:

bit.ly/2aAmtgM

OTHER IDEAS

• Leave a note on your kids' pillows, so when they go to bed they'll find them. Tell them to meet you at the car at a certain time with their pillow and blanket, and then surprise them with a night of lights. If they're old enough to not spill in the car, you can bring along hot chocolate to keep you warm. Or, you can make a hot chocolate stop before you head home! If your kids aren't quite old enough to read, then you can just tell them to grab their pillows and meet you at the car. Sometimes if we really want to surprise them, we'll do it on a school night!

• Visit a local museum or site that's having a special lights display or show. When we lived in Texas, our local zoo had an incredible lights display, and it was a tradition that we had while we lived there.

• Research neighboring towns or neighborhoods that are known for their light displays, and then take your family to see it! We've lucked out in all the places we've lived, because we've always been able to find something special to go see.

christmas Lights scavenger hunt

☐ reindeer ☐ christmas
☐ snowman ☐ penguin
☐ santa claus ☐ mrs. claus
☐ nutcracker ☐ snowflake
☐ candy cane ☐ snowglobe
☐ twinkling lights ☐ train
☐ ice skates ☐ santa's sleigh
☐ gingerbread ☐ blue lights
☐ manger scene ☐ angel
☐ santa's elves ☐ carolers

christmas Lights scavenger hunt *for kids*

 reindeer   ice skates
snowman   gingerbread
santa claus   manger scene
nutcracker   santa's elves
candy cane   penguin
train   christmas tree

LETTERS TO SANTA. . . AND GETTING A REPLY!

The motto in our house is "if you don't believe, you don't receive," and so yes, we all believe in Santa Claus. We believe in him and what he stands for—goodness, giving, generosity, kindness, and thinking of others first.

Because of this, he sprinkles a lot of magic into the Christmas season, and writing letters to Santa has been a tradition since our oldest was little. We save a special night at the beginning of December—usually our family night—just for our letter writing. It's most assuredly accompanied by hot chocolate and popcorn, and we sit down together to write.

I've always loved seeing what kinds of things they write in their letters, and how it changes over the years. I have boys that are in kindergarten this year, and just learning how to write words and sentences. Isn't there something so adorable about those backward s's and crooked letters? As they get older, there's something just as precious in the beginning cursive. Their individual personalities shine through, and it's so fun to see what they write.

While we've always mailed our letters after they're written, several years ago I stumbled upon the secret to receiving a reply from Santa himself! I'll tell you, it's a very exciting day for little people, when the mail comes and there's a letter to them bearing the North Pole seal, and a return address that reads "SANTA CLAUS"!

I've got all the information here for you, plus some adorable "Dear Santa" stationery to write letters on! Each of these places accept letters from all over the world, so no matter where you live, your kids can write letters to Santa Claus.

· · · · · ·

SANTA CLAUS, INDIANA

I received a note from the Director of the Santa Claus Museum and Village and she gives details on letters to and from Santa. In addition to our donation, I also include stamps for each letter.

Hi All,

Merry Christmas! I am the Director at the Santa Claus Museum and Village and one of Santa's Elves. I just wanted to encourage everyone to get those letters in by December 20—the earlier, the better! The Elves get pretty overwhelmed close to the deadline. We do try to respond to every child who sends a letter, though sometimes there are problems if the return address is not legible. So make sure there is a clear return address listed. And these letters are all free, though we certainly welcome donations!

We're a small non-profit organization with volunteer Elves, and every little bit helps. If you have any questions or need more information, check out our website at **www.santaclausmuseum.org/letters-to-santa/** There is also a link for "print at home" letters if you would prefer to do that rather than mail a letter to us. You can also give us a call at 812-544-2434.

**Santa Claus
P.O. Box 1
Santa Claus, IN
47579**

Santa

really
remote
controlled
stuffed
animal dog

Love,

Henry

santa c
P.O. Bo
santa cla

CANADA POST

Checklist from their website: **bit.ly/1MQc9ll**

· Postage isn't required for the return letter—they want every child to get a letter back! (I'm sure if you wanted to include extra stamps, they would love that too!)

· Mail your letters by December 16th.

· Make sure to include your full return address. Santa's address is

Santa Claus, North Pole
HOH OHO, CANADA

ROYAL MAIL/UK

Checklist from their website:
www.royalmail.com/letters-to-santa

· Mail your letters by December 6th

· Make sure your letter is stamped, and includes child's full name and address

Santa/Father Christmas
Santa's Grotto,
Reindeerland,
XM4 5HQ

If you want to just send a letter to Santa (with no reply), here are a few address options:

Santa Claus
North Pole,
Alaska 99705

Santa Claus
North Pole,
New York, 12946

Last minute letters can be sent via e-mail, at
www.emailsanta.com.

To download the Santa stationery, enter the following URL into your computer's address bar.

Stationary with Rudolph:

bit.ly/2beMlAm

Stationary with Santa:

bit.ly/2aGURw7

Stationary with Christmas Tree:

bit.ly/2aMywLd

FAMILY BOOK EXCHANGE

Books are a big part of not just Christmas at our house, but the whole year. When it comes time to write letters to Santa, books are at the top of everyone's Christmas list. As an avid reader, it makes my heart happy that my kids love books so much too.

I've hosted and participated in many Christmas book exchanges with friends and book clubs over the years, but this past year it hit me . . . how fun it would be to have a family Christmas book exchange! A few weeks before Christmas, we all picked names out of a hat. We would buy a book for that person, and though it was supposed to be a secret, that's usually easier said than done, especially with little ones that are just bursting with eagerness! We set a reasonable budget, considering the ages of our kids, and how much money they would be able to earn. All the kids had opportunities to earn money along the way by doing extra chores around the house, and they could also use any savings they already had.

Each child could consult with mom and dad about ideas, but in the end, they got to make the final decision on their own about which book was just the right one. It was so fun to hear them so excited about it, and to talk about what their person would love . . . and why. My husband and I spent time with each child to help them make their purchase—sometimes it was at the bookstore, and often times we spent time perusing online resources, looking at all the options and making our purchase there. It was a really fun way to spend time with each child alone, and an extra benefit of this new tradition.

We decided on Christmas Eve as the night for our book party, and thought it would be the perfect addition to our Christmas Eve "lineup." We went one-by-one starting with the smallest, each person opening up their book, then in turn, handing over their gift to the next in line. The laughter and squeals of excitement to both give and receive were the icing on the cake.

Our first annual family book exchange was a bona fide hit, and is now a tradition that will be a part of our family for many Christmases to come.

· · · · · ·

My favorite Christmas tradition is something my husband's parents did when their children were young. They didn't want the kids getting up too early to see what their presents were, so they set booby traps to keep them in their rooms longer. They hung string all over their rooms with bells on it. They set up containers of marbles that would dump into metal bowls when doors were opened. They even wrapped the opening to the hallway with wrapping paper and tape. We started doing booby traps with our kids last Christmas. We hung string across the basement where they were sleeping, and covered the stairs in cardboard so they couldn't climb up. We also had marbles come rolling down the cardboard as they tried to climb up. They had so much fun they asked if we would do it again this year.

The Rice Family | Utah

THE TIMELESS CLASS

WITH FOREWORDS BY JUDY

ANN M. MARTIN & JOHANNA HUR

The Betsy-Tacy Treasur

Betsy-Tacy

Betsy-Tacy a

d Tacy Go Downtown

MAUD HART L

ILLUSTRATED BY

The First Four B

HARPERPERENNIA

CHRISTMAS CARD ASSEMBLY LINE

I love sending and receiving Christmas cards. Despite the introduction of social media, and the fact that with Facebook and Instagram we can regularly connect with friends and family, I still prefer a tangible version. We hang them on a twine garland over the doorway, or clip them up on a chicken wire frame on the wall, or even punch holes in one corner and slide them on to a book ring. It's so fun to be able to glance at them the entire holiday season, and my kids will sit down several times and look through them over and over again. They love to ask questions about each family—how they know them, how long they've known them, and where they live. Needless to say, we love checking the mail in November and December!

We send cards out ever year, and as we've moved around the country, we've collected wonderful friends, and our list has grown. Several years ago, when my girls were just tiny, they begged to help me put everything together. I took them up on it, and ever since then, we've had our own little Christmas card assembly line!

It's now a full-fledged Wade family Christmas tradition, and all of our kids absolutely love to help get the Christmas cards ready to send out. Even the youngest gets to help, and last Christmas, when my baby was 18-months old, she was a part of it! We sit around the kitchen table, and around we go! We have a stuffer, two labelers—one for our address, and one for the recipient's address—someone to lick the envelope flap, a stamp placer, and, finally, someone to add a cute piece of washi tape on the back! My husband and I help the littlest ones, and in less than hour (usually 30–40 minutes), more than 100 Christmas cards are ready to go!

Oh, the conversations we have while we're working together! I laugh just thinking back on them. To have that time together, just talking, working, and listening to Christmas music—it's priceless. Not only does it save me a ton of time, but the kids get to know they're contributing, and we get valuable family time.

After we're finished, tradition calls for homemade hot chocolate and cookies. Of course.

. . . . . .

To create your own Christmas card assembly line, set a night aside on your calendar so you can be prepared. We have a weekly Family Night, so that particular evening always works well for us.

Gather everything ahead of time, and set them out: stamps, envelopes, cards, return address stamp or labels, printed address labels, pens, and a little bowl of water and sponge in case the licking gives out. And even a little washi tape for decoration if you want to!

Assign everyone a job, based on age and/or ability. When we had fewer children, my husband and I would double or triple up on jobs.

You can make it part of the adventure to take all of your cards to the post office or place them in your mailbox!

TIP: Several years ago, I typed up all of the addresses of our friends and family in a Word label document. I make updates as necessary when people move or change names. When it's time for Christmas cards, all I have to do is print them onto labels. It saves so much time compared to writing all the addresses out. It might take a while to type them up, but you only have to do it once and then you're done!

A FIRE STATION THANK YOU

Sunday afternoons were spent at the nursing home during my growing up years, and I'm full of memories there—singing, playing the piano, talking, and spending time with the patients. Oh, the stories they could (and did) tell! It was always an adventure, and I learned a lot about life, compassion, and other people.

My parents were really good about giving us opportunities to serve, and I learned at a young age how important it is to give, to think outside yourself, and to show gratitude for what you've been given. I'm grateful for those experiences, and I'm really hoping to pass that along to my own children. A few Christmases ago, I made a giving list—a list of ideas and ways our little family could serve others, and spread a little cheer and gratitude to those that serve us. I really wanted to focus

my children and family on serving more, giving more, and reaching out more to others in our community.

One of the things we had on our giving list was to visit the fire station, bring treats to the firefighters there, and thank them for their service to our neighborhood and community. This was a natural for our family—my two boys were and still are OBSESSED with anything fireman related, including fire stations, fire fighters, fire trucks, and last but not least, "fire dogs."

One evening we made thank you cards, bags of yummy treats, and headed over to our local fire station to deliver them. We rang the doorbell, and the sign above it said that 911 would be called if they didn't answer in 20 seconds! We were hoping they would be really

fast . . . and they were. They came over an intercom to talk to us, and when we said we had treats, they were up front to answer the door in less than 30 seconds!

They were thrilled to see the kids there, and gave them the royal treatment. The letters we wrote went up on their fridge in the kitchen, and we got to spend awhile exploring all the fire engines. We had quite a few firefighters come out and talk to us and and the kids. It was so enjoyable to spend time with them, find out more about them, and thank them for their service and what they bring to our neighborhood and community. It was one of the best nights, and we all left so happy and full of the spirit of Christmas. They told us to come back anytime, and we happily decided that it was a tradition that should and would be continued.

· · · · · ·

- You many want to call ahead to the fire station to check to see if they have specific visiting hours.
- If your child can write, give them the opportunity to write their own letter. It's so fun to see what they want to say, and how they say it. I like to take a picture of their letters before we go, so I have a record of them.
- I've created fun fire truck stationery, and you can download the fire station thank you letter by typing in the following link into your computer's address bar, then saving to your computer and printing onto white paper.

bit.ly/2b8EiWy

CHRISTMAS SING-ALONG

When we received the invitation to our first Christmas sing-along, we accepted wholeheartedly. We had just moved to a new town for our first job out of graduate school and we were looking forward to meeting new friends. With all of our family thousands of miles away, we were especially glad to enjoy the holidays with other families.

It really was a perfect evening. Nothing fancy—just a bunch of families gathered around the piano singing Christmas songs, munching on yummy Christmas treats spread out on the kitchen table, and enjoying each other's company. Our son was in heaven playing with all of the other kids, and we spent several wonderful hours there. Too soon it was time to say good-bye. Lifelong friendships began to form that night, and it's still one of our most memorable holiday parties to date.

I knew it was going to be something I would enjoy—as a pianist, music has long been my passion. But my husband, who never sings except for the hymns at church (and when he's been cajoled into it by our little ones over the years, and singing lullabies to babies when he thinks no one else can hear), absolutely loved it. Since that first year, he has been the driving force behind

hosting our own Christmas sing-alongs, and is one of his main requests every year. You don't have to be really good at singing to enjoy a Christmas sing-along. You just have to love Christmas and being together with friends and family!

I love this particular tradition because amidst everything going on during the holidays, it's a gathering that doesn't need a lot of time to plan or prepare. It can also be spontaneous if you end up with a free night and want to have people over. We've even decided on a Sunday to invite people over that night!

Make it simple—invite friends and family, pop some popcorn, make a batch of hot chocolate, or even ask everyone to bring a favorite treat or appetizer. If you don't have a piano, make a fun playlist and sing to that! My very favorite book of Christmas songs is the Reader's Digest Christmas Songbook. It has every Christmas song you can imagine, both religious and secular, and even comes with a book containing lyrics only, so your guests can see the words while they sing.

No matter how you do it, gathering around to sing and celebrate the most wonderful time of the year is the perfect way to bring in the spirit of Christmas!

CHRISTMAS BAKING DAY

The kitchen is truly the heart of our home. We spend so much time in the kitchen together as a family—cooking, baking, gathering around the table for meals, playing games, eating a midnight snack, doing homework, and so much more. During the holidays it's even more so that way, and when friends and family come to visit, the kitchen is where we gather. The kitchen is even more magical during the holiday season. So many yummy smells emanating from that part of the house, not to mention the warmth of the oven.

My kids absolutely love to be in the kitchen with me, and helping in any way I'll let them. They also know there's usually a payoff involved, in the form of licking the spoon or getting a few extra chocolate chips! I knew that they would especially love it if they all got plenty of time to help, with lots of different projects to work on together. With so much Christmas baking to do, all of these things seemed to meld together, and a Family Christmas Baking Day was born.

How does it work? After getting input from everyone, and deciding on what we're doing for neighbor gifts, I make a list of all the baking I want and need to do and I gather all the supplies ahead of time. I also map out what needs to be done, and an order that makes the most sense—based on what needs the oven and what doesn't. We designate a day (usually a Saturday, or even Sunday if we have an early church meeting time), write it on the calendar, and make sure we set that time aside.

Then . . . we get to work. Christmas music goes on, and the fun begins! I have the best helpers—they love to stir, measure and pour in ingredients, use the mixer, and they are the best at unwrapping candies. It does take

longer, but that's okay—I know it's going to, and being together is the most important part of the day.

With a very young family, often the baking "day" is not really a full day, or even close to it—and that's okay. As the years go by and the kids get older, that will change, and they will gradually be able to do more and more. For right now, we do as much as we can together, then I finish up what's left.

At the end of the day, we've accomplished a lot—usually just about everything is done that needs to be. We've got friend and neighbor gifts set to go, and we've done it together.

Baking day is also a really fun tradition to have with friends. One of my most favorite (and funniest) Christmas memories is a baking night I had with my some of my best friends. We decided that we would each bring a new recipe to try, and then we would divide them up to take home with us when we were finished. It all failed spectacularly, and not one recipe looked like it was supposed to (even though they did taste good). It will always be a memory I treasure!

Some of our favorite Christmas recipes were inherited from my grandmother, who was an incredible Southern cook and baker. When I was little, the most anticipated package of the whole Christmas season came from her, and it was always chock full of delicious Christmas goodies. I don't think they lasted more than an hour! My mouth is watering just thinking about it! Others have been passed down from my mom, and shared by friends.

Happy Baking!

· · · · · ·

PECAN TASSIES

I love the rich crust paired with the crunch of toasted pecans! These little cookies are rich and delicious, and have always been a favorite of mine. Especially the ones my grandma made.

· · · · · ·

INGREDIENTS

1 (3 oz.) pkg. cream cheese

½ cup butter

1 cup sifted all-purpose flour

1 egg

¾ cup brown sugar

1 Tbsp. soft butter

1 tsp. vanilla

dash salt

½ cup ground pecans

DIRECTIONS

· Blend the softened cream cheese and butter. Stir in flour. Chill 1 hour.

· Shape into 2 dozen 1" balls. Place in ungreased 1¾ inch muffin tins. Press dough in bottoms and up sides. Prepare filling.

· Beat together egg, brown sugar, butter, vanilla, and salt. Add ground pecans and mix well.

· Evenly distribute pecan mixture among the pastry-lined pans. Bake at 325 degrees for 25 minutes. or until the filling is set. Cool before removing from pans.

On Christmas Eve we have a traditional Israelite dinner, eating the things that Jesus might have eaten. It's probably not completely accurate but we do our best: dried apricots and dates and figs, apples, grapes, pomegranate, olives, pita chips, rustic bread, olive oil, goat cheese, and beef jerky. It's easy to prepare and helps us to focus on Christ on a night when it's easy to get caught up in all the presents and last minute preparations.

The Wrights | West Virginia

SNOWBALL COOKIES

These yummy, cookies were called Walnut Crescents by my grandmother, who shaped hers into crescent shapes. I decided to make mine round, but no matter what you call them, or what shape they are, they are buttery, melt-in-your-mouth goodness!

· · · · · ·

INGREDIENTS

2 cups unsifted flour

1 cup soft butter

¼ cup powdered sugar

2 Tbsp. cold water

2 tsp. vanilla

⅔ cup chopped walnuts

DIRECTIONS

· Beat sugar and butter together. Add flour and water alternately. Add vanilla and walnuts. Mix well and shape into crescent shapes and bake about 15 minutes at 350 degrees.

· Sift powdered sugar on cutting board. Place baked cookies on sugar immediately out of oven and sift sugar over each cookie. Makes about 6 dozen.

A Christmas tradition we have at the Madsen house is that of including in our row of hung stockings, a white stocking for Jesus. Each year we write on a piece of paper something we would like to give the Savior such as a kinder heart toward our friends and family, a more faithful study of the scriptures, or the elimination of a habit we know we should change. We put the slips of paper in the white stocking. On the next Christmas Eve, we take the stocking down and read the gifts we gave Jesus the year before. We read them to ourselves and assess how we did. Then we write a new goal or promise, and commit it to Him. It is really the only gift we can give Him that He doesn't already have.

The Madsen Family | Utah

CARAMEL NUT MARSHMALLOWS

These were in the Christmas package my grandma sent, and all of my siblings and I would fight over them. The caramel and nuts combined with the marshmallow is a winning combination, and they're so cute served on lollipop sticks or paper straws cut into half!

· · · · · ·

INGREDIENTS

1 package large marshmallows

1 lb. package Kraft caramels

¾ cup half and half

finely chopped pecans or walnuts

lollipop sticks

DIRECTIONS

· Put marshmallows onto the lollipop sticks. Place the nuts in a pie plate or other shallow dish.

· Heat caramel and half and half very slowly until thoroughly melted and smooth. Dip the marshmallows one by one into the caramel, and then roll in the nuts.

· Place them on wax paper, and let the caramel set for at least an hour before serving.

We asked each of our children and their families, to focus on acts of service throughout the year rather than purchasing gifts for Cecil and me. On Christmas Eve they each share what service they gave. They tell how it helped them to focus on the Savior throughout the year and how it made them feel.

The Place Family | Michigan

NO-COOK FUDGE

I love fudge, and this no-cook recipe is quick and simple! It melts in your mouth, and is absolutely mouthwatering!

. . . . . .

INGREDIENTS

½ cup butter

3 oz. cream cheese

3½ cup powdered sugar

¼ cup cocoa

1 tsp. vanilla

nuts (optional)

DIRECTIONS

· Mix all the ingredients together until a ball is formed. If I'm adding nuts, I'll mix all the ingredients together except the nuts, then mix them in at the end.

· Using your hands is the easiest way to get it all mixed really well! Roll into two rolls, each 1" thick.

· Wrap in plastic wrap. You can also place it in a glass dish that's been lined with plastic wrap or wax paper. Refrigerate until firm enough to slice or cut into squares.

My husband and I both grew up playing chimes with our families every year for Christmas. A few years ago we asked my husband's father, who is very handy, to make us our own set of chimes. It is now one of our favorite traditions to invite several families over the weeks leading up to Christmas and play chimes. We call it Chimes & Pie because the first year we did it we ate pie for dessert, so, now it has become a tradition.

The Carn Family | Michigan

CARAMELS

This recipe is from my mom, and a family favorite. I adore caramels, and these are rich, buttery, chewy perfection.

· · · · · ·

INGREDIENTS

1 cup sugar

1 cup Karo syrup (corn syrup)

1 cup heavy cream

1½ Tbsp. butter

1 Tbsp. vanilla

chopped pecans or walnuts (optional)

DIRECTIONS

· Mix sugar, corn syrup, butter, and half of the cream. Bring to a boil. Add the rest of the cream slowly so the boiling does not stop.

· Cook to a firm ball—halfway between soft and hard, between 240–250 degrees on a candy thermometer.

· Remove from heat. Add vanilla and nuts. Pour into a buttered pan and cool. Cut into small pieces and wrap in wax paper, twisting the ends.

On Christmas morning when I was a child, everyone was rushing to open their gifts and we would often miss seeing what everyone else was receiving. To slow things down and enjoy Christmas more my mom came up with this idea. We would draw one another's names and shop for one of our siblings. We would then be responsible to create a scavenger hunt for the person for whom we bought the gift. The gift would be found at the end of the scavenger hunt. This would be anything from written out clues, picture clues, and even sometimes sound clues. We would then open these gifts one at a time to enjoy, to see what was given, and where it had been hidden. The scavenger hunt competition of seeing who could create the craziest hunt was always a part of the fun. As we got older, the clues became more elaborate and the gifts were hidden in even more crazy places. The best part is that this tradition has continued for over 30 years and is now carried out by each cousin drawing each other's names and creating the scavenger hunts for each other. There are 27 cousins so you can imagine the crazy, fun holiday party this is each year! My mom was able to accomplish her goal of "slowing down" Christmas and creating a fun way for children to enjoy gift giving.

The Callahan Family | Utah

ENGLISH TOFFEE BARS

A rich crust covered in toffee and chocolate—what's not to love?

• • • • • •

INGREDIENTS

2⅓ cup flour

⅔ cup brown sugar

2 cups chocolate chips

14 oz. can sweetened condensed milk

¾ cup butter

1 egg, slightly beaten

1 cup coarsely chopped nuts (pecans or walnuts)

1¾ cup toffee bits (10 oz.)

DIRECTIONS

· Preheat oven to 350 degrees. In a large bowl mix the flour and sugar together. Cut in butter until the mixture is coarse crumbs, Add beaten egg and mix well.

· Stir in 1½ cups chocolate chips and nuts. Reserve 1½ cups of that mixture. Press the rest into a greased 9 x 13 pan. Bake for 10 minutes. Pour the sweetened condensed milk over the top in an even layer. Top with 1½ cups toffee bits. Sprinkle reserved crumb mixture on top, followed by the remaining chocolate chips.

· Bake 25–30 minutes or until golden brown. Sprinkle remaining toffee bits on top, then cool completely before cutting into bars.

My grandparents were children of first generation German parents. They had a tradition in their home in which the parents hid a pickle ornament in the branches of the Christmas tree as they decorated it. Whoever found the pickle ornament on Christmas Eve got an extra present. Christmas Eve was the day they always decorated for Christmas and exchanged gifts. When I was a child, we opened all of our family presents on Christmas Eve, and then would have a Santa gift to open on Christmas Day. My husband and I chose to modify my German family traditions a little. We put up our Christmas tree the day after Thanksgiving. We hide a pickle ornament and whoever finds it gets to put on the Christmas star. We open one present on Christmas Eve and the rest are opened on Christmas Day.

The Harsch Family | Texas

CHOCOLATE PEPPERMINT BLOSSOMS

Oh, how I love chocolate and peppermint together. They are the perfect Christmas combination. My kids love to help with this recipe, and unwrap all of the peppermint kisses for me. It's probably because I let them do a little sampling as payment!

· · · · · ·

INGREDIENTS

1 cup softened butter

1 cup white sugar

1 cup packed brown sugar

2 eggs

2¼ cups flour

¾ cup cocoa

2 tsp. vanilla

1 tsp. baking soda

1–2 Tbsp. white sugar

36 Candy Cane Hershey's Kisses

DIRECTIONS

· Beat butter until creamy, then add sugars. Beat in eggs and vanilla. Combine flour, soda, and cocoa, then add to the butter mixture, beating well.

· Roll into small balls, then into the 1–2 Tbsp. white sugar. Place on a cookie sheet lined with parchment paper or foil and sprayed with cooking spray. Bake for 7–8 minutes at 375 degrees. If your oven tends to bake quickly, check them around 6 minutes—don't overbake!

· As soon as they come out of the oven, press a Candy Cane kiss in the center of each cookie. Remove the cookies from the cookie sheet as soon as possible, so the kisses don't melt.

My favorite Christmas tradition is buying a new family ornament each year, one that represents something significant that has happened in our lives during the past year. As we put up the Christmas tree, we pull out each ornament and tell the story behind it. By the time we have finished, we have told the history of our family, from marriage to the birth of each child, the adoption of each pet, the purchase of each house, special vacations and other memorable events. Choosing an ornament each year is a special occurrence as we debate which ornament is worthy that year. We all look forward to it, especially the kids. They love to hear how each story weaves together to tell the history of our little family.

The Durrant Family | Utah

THE GIRLS & THE NUTCRACKER BALLET

There are very good reasons why I never became a ballerina. Mostly it's because after trying to dance to "Uptown Girl" in my first ever dance recital, and not having any clue what I was doing, I realized that my heart was on the soccer field, and not a dance stage. I have still retained a deep appreciation for dance, and as a musician, have always loved the cultural arts.

Long ago, I remember reading a book where the mom always took her girls to see the Nutcracker Ballet each Christmas season. I decided that when and if I had girls of my own, that's what I would do. It was many years later that my twin girls were born, and that stuck with me.

When they were three years old, the Nutcracker came to our local center for the arts, and I was SO excited to start the tradition with them. They were equally as thrilled to get dressed up, go to lunch, and then attend the matinee performance. It's a very long production, and so I wasn't surprised that we didn't make it the whole time, but it was okay, and we all had a wonderful day. Every year since then, we have gone every year to a production of the Nutcracker ballet at Christmastime.

Sometimes it's a professional performance, and other years, when that hasn't been available, or sometimes for the sake of ease, scheduling, or budget, we've attended productions by local dance companies. One of my girls is now taking ballet, and hopes that one year we'll be watching her dance in it! One Christmas my mom was in town, and she was able to come as well—it was so fun to have her with us!

We still get dressed up, and always go to a "fancy" lunch or dinner first. Talking, laughing, being together—those are the best traditions of all! We've added one more little girl to our family, and soon enough she'll be able to join us too. The boys have their own night—usually pizza and football—and pretty much eating anything they want because mom isn't home!

Music is such an integral part of the Christmas season. You can't go anywhere, even the grocery store, without hearing strains of "Jingle Bells" or "Joy to the World" and I love it! It's one of the best parts of Christmas, and whether it's a play, ballet, or concert, enjoying Christmas music together is a wonderful tradition.

· · · · · ·

DETAILS

- Most communities will host Christmas concerts or other musical events during the holidays. Some of our favorite Christmas memories include musical Christmas walks at our local library, downtown area, and even the zoo! Ask friends and neighbors for recommendations, and check your local newspaper for a list of upcoming musical events.

- If you're interested in seeing The Nutcracker, check local ballet companies as well as a professional dance company, if you have one in your area. The professional performances will be a lot more expensive, so if it doesn't fit your budget, or your kids are young, I suggest trying a local company instead.

SNOWMAN SOUP

Creating small treats and gifts for our neighbors together has been a family tradition since the very beginning. My kids have always loved to be a part of things, and I've always loved not only the help, but the company too! We also make the deliveries together—we pile in the car, turn on the Christmas music, and enjoy driving around our town and area to drop everything off.

We do something different every year, but there are a few things that we like to repeat, because we love them so much. One of those is Snowman Soup, a definite favorite over the years. They're super easy to put together, so if you're not up for baking, or are short on time, it's a perfect solution. They're easily tailored for an individual or a family, which makes them great for neighbors, friends, teachers, colleagues, bus drivers, and more. Plus . . . they're super CUTE!

All you need are mini marshmallows, mini candy canes, and hot chocolate packet to create the soup, plus adorable printable I've created for you and something to put it all in.

If I'm making one for a family, I like to use brown paper sacks, because they're inexpensive, hold quite a bit, and look really cute tied up with ribbon or baker's twine. When I'm making individual sizes, I've used paper treat bags, clear treat bags, takeout boxes, round paper ice cream containers, and mason jars. Creating an assembly line is a great way to make Snowman Soup—and a great way for a family to work together!

· · · · · ·

FOR EACH SNOWMAN SOUP SERVING, YOU'LL NEED

- Place a handful of mini marshmallows in a plastic snack bag. I also like to cut off the top of a sandwich bag, place the marshmallows inside, and tie it shut with baker's twine or ribbon. If I'm using mason jars, I just place the marshmallows directly in the jar.
- For each serving, place a bag of marshmallows, candy cane(s), and a hot chocolate packet in the container you're using. If I'm creating a family packet, I'll put as many in as there are members of the family.
- Use ribbon, baker's twine, jute, or fabric strips to close or embellish your container.

To download the Snowman Soup printable, enter the one of the following urls in the address bar of your computer, and then save. Print onto white cardstock. I like to snip the ends on each side so it looks like a tag!

bit.ly/2aHiTmF

INGREDIENTS

one hot chocolate mix
packet
mini candy canes
or peppermint
chocolate kisses
a little packet of mini
marshmallows
something to put it in
(see above ideas)
printable (link to
download below)

THE RING-AND-RUN DINNER

Camille Adamson Beckstrand, sixsisterstuff.com

For as long as I can remember, my parents made the Christmas season all about helping others. Each holiday season, we would choose one family in our area who had had a tough year or who could use a little bit of help.

Choosing the family was half the fun; all year we would keep our eyes open for someone that we thought would be the perfect people to help and many times it took a little bit of detective work. Sometimes it would a kid from school, sometimes it was people from our church, sometimes it was someone we knew about in the community who had come on hard times, and sometimes it was my parents' co-workers. We never had a lot of extra money growing up, but even with the little that we did have, our parents taught us to share.

Once the family was chosen, we would all go to the grocery store together and purchase everything that was needed for a big Christmas dinner—a turkey or ham, potatoes, green beans, gravy, stuffing, pumpkin pie, etc. We would also purchase just some other food staples or things that family might need and throw all the groceries together all in a big box. If we knew more about the family's specific needs, we would purchase a few items or small toys if they had children.

 On Christmas Eve night, around 8 or 9 pm, we would pause our Christmas Eve party and load the big box of food into the family van. We would drive to the family's house that we had picked and scope out the area so we could plan our secret getaway. We then chose two people to carry the heavy box of food and gifts to the door. Once they set the box on the porch, they had to do the classic "Ring and Run"—ring the doorbell, then run back to the car as fast as their legs would carry them! When we were little, it was usually our mom and dad that would do the ringing and running, but as my sisters and I got older (and faster than our parents!), we were able to take turns dropping off the box and running away. The getaway car was usually parked around the corner and sometimes you had to run far to make it back to the car. I don't think that we have ever been caught, but we have definitely had some close calls!

Once the runners were safely back in the car, we would usually drive around the block for a couple of minutes and then drive past the house again to make sure the family got their box. Our adrenaline is always pumping by this point . . . there is something so exciting about being secretive! Some of my favorite memories are the drive home after finishing another successful Ring-and-Run and talking about the close calls of being caught and wondering about the family who had just received a fun Christmas gift. Receiving gifts is wonderful, but giving away gifts—especially secret ones—is what makes the holidays even more special.

Out of all our family traditions, this is definitely the one that we look forward to the most and one that we have continued to do for more than 25 years.

• • • • • •

REINDEER PANCAKES

For our family, something that sets apart the holidays from regular days is extra special breakfasts. At Christmastime, that means Reindeer Pancakes, and our kids absolutely love them. We like to make them on Christmas Eve morning—they're festive and fun, and perfect for the day before Christmas. Cute bacon antlers, a strawberry for the nose, blueberry eyes, and dollops of whipped cream to hold it all together go on two pancakes to create the cutest and yummiest reindeer ever!

• • • • • •

INGREDIENTS

pancakes: half of
    them a little
    bigger, and the
    other half a little
    smaller
spray whipped cream
strawberries, whole
    and hulled
blueberries
bacon

DIRECTIONS

· Lay one larger pancake on the plate, and then place one of the smaller pancakes on top, toward the bottom of the larger one.
· Add dollops of whipped cream for the eyes and the nose, then put the berries on top—blueberries for the eyes, and a strawberry for the nose. Break the bacon into pieces, and use two for each antler, angling them outward.

A TRADITION WITH MY HUSBAND:
WRAPPING PRESENTS ON CHRISTMAS EVE

Those who know me in real life are flabbergasted that we still do this. I'm an organizer and a planner that doesn't like to leave anything to the last minute. If there is anything crazier than wrapping all of the Christmas presents for all of your six kids the night before Christmas . . . I don't know what is!

It all started when were first married. We were living in student housing, working hard at our jobs, and studying a lot. We didn't have much money for gifts, or really much time to do any shopping, so the one gift we got for each other we wrapped on Christmas Eve (separately) and put under the tree for the next morning.

A few years later when our son was born, we were still students and working. We wrapped all of his presents together on Christmas Eve while watching one of our favorite Christmas movies, then placed them under the tree. He was only three months old, and had just a few presents, so it didn't take long at all! We drank hot chocolate, finished our movie, and that became our own little Christmas Eve tradition. For nearly eight more years, our son was our only child so it was easy to do, and since we loved it so much, the tradition continued.

After eight long years of infertility, we felt very grateful and so lucky to have five children in the next six years, including two sets of twins. To say our life changed is an understatement—we suddenly had five car seats, lots of diapers to change, and quite a few more Christmas presents! Those first years are still quite a blur, to be honest, and our Christmas Eve wrapping tradition was actually its own blessing.

It's now a couple of years down the road, and we've graduated to only three car seats, and one in diapers. And when it comes to our Christmas Eve tradition of wrapping all the presents together, it's become one of our favorite parts of the Christmas season. We have a three present per child limit, and between the two of us, we're pretty fast! Last Christmas we were finished wrapping and in bed by 10:00 pm!

But truly, it's SO fun for us. The kids are tucked snugly in their beds, there's a pile of presents and rolls and rolls of wrapping paper and bows between us, we have mugs of piping hot chocolate and one of our favorite Christmas movies is playing. It's our own little Christmas party together, and we cherish it and look forward to it ever year. It was an accidental tradition, and I'm so glad for it.

· · · · · ·

Photo Credit www.stephanielowephotography.com

CHRISTMAS EVE NATIVITY

Reading the story of the birth of Christ in the Bible is the last thing we do on Christmas Eve before the kids go to bed. Yes, there is excitement in the air about Santa Claus coming, but we want the last thoughts of Christmas to be about our Savior, Jesus Christ—He is the real reason we are celebrating, and the true focus of the entire Christmas season. So, after checking where Santa currently is on his trek across the world, after reading *The Night Before Christmas*, and after leaving sugar and carrots for the reindeer and cookies for Santa, we settle down for the story of how it all began.

Since our oldest was tiny, we've acted out the Nativity while reading. It has provided us many, many memorable moments over the years, including some of the funniest. I know, maybe that's not quite how we intended it to be, but with little kids, you just never know what's going to happen—and I love it. That's how memories are made!

Everyone has a part, and while we've tried to mix things up, our kids have their favorites, so we tend to keep them the same from year to year. We don't have fancy costumes—we've discovered that hand towels held in place with running headbands work perfectly for the shepherds, innkeeper, and Joseph; a white sheet and a bit of tinsel are just right for the angel; and a large towel to drape over her head is exactly what Mary needs.

We have a lot of "stuffies" (stuffed animals) to play the parts of the animals and anyone else we've been missing over the years. We had one child for a long time, so he got to play whatever part he wanted, then the stuffed animals filled in the rest. With six kids now, we've got a Mary, Joseph, angel, innkeeper, shepherd, and often times a baby Jesus. My husband has been the donkey that carries Mary into Bethlehem, but now that my oldest son is a teenager, he's filling that role. I'm the narrator and videographer, and my husband helps everyone get to where they need to be.

What I love most are the questions and discoveries that it brings—before, after, and sometimes even during our reenactment. Through acting it out, they get a very small glimpse into what the night might have been like, and we get to spend some time talking about it. I can see the wheels turning in their little heads, and their sweet little comments touch me like nothing else can. It's a treasured Christmas Eve tradition, and one to be carried on for generations to come!

• • • • • •

Photo Credit by www.ccmcafeeperspective.com

GERMAN PANCAKES

One of the things I remember most about my childhood Christmases is German Pancakes. We had them only once a year for our Christmas breakfast, and it was something we talked about and literally looked forward to the entire year.

We would wake up super early (of course), and once we woke my parents up, were able to look at our stockings to see what Santa brought. He was always very generous in those stockings, and examining the contents were what held our patience a little longer while my parents made our yummy breakfast.

When it was finally time to eat—it always seemed to take forever as a child—we smothered the German Pancakes in real whipped cream, and piled on high the blueberries, strawberries, and raspberries. It's still my favorite way to eat them! I don't even know how many

pans of them my mom and dad had to make, because boy, could we make them disappear!

After breakfast was over, we opened our presents one at a time, and enjoyed the rest of the morning together. It was a special way to celebrate Christmas, and I loved every minute of it.

When I got married, that was a tradition that I knew I wanted to continue, and now my own kids love German Pancakes as much as I do. I serve them the same way, and we still eat breakfast before opening our presents— but after stockings.

My kids love hearing about my childhood Christmases, and I love telling them. It's especially fun when certain traditions are carried over, and we have a connection from generation to generation.

· · · · · ·

INGREDIENTS

5 eggs
1 cup flour
½ cup cornmeal
1 cup buttermilk
1 cup milk
¼ cup butter
heavy cream
powdered sugar

DIRECTIONS

· Preheat oven to 425 degrees. Lightly beat eggs, and then add sifted flour, cornmeal, buttermilk and milk. Beat 5 minutes. I often use the blender to mix everything.

· Melt butter in a 9 x 13 baking dish in the oven. Pour in batter and bake for 25 minutes until lightly browned!

· Beat heavy cream until soft peaks form, then add powdered sugar to sweeten. Serve with whipped cream and berries!

A Christmas Tradition that our family loves is our "Candy Sled Races". We decorate 4.4 oz. Hershey or Symphony Bars to look like sleds. We wrap the bar in Christmas paper, then we hot glue two candy canes (leaving the plastic on the candy canes!) to the bottom of the candy bar. The rounded part of the candy cane comes around and up over the front of the candy bar and those are the "blades". We then hot glue as many Christmas toys and candies to the top as desired. Let me tell you, there is a lot of conversation about weight distribution, drag and aerodynamic strategies going on while the MEN are creating their sleds. The competition is tough! We then stretch a heavy plastic tarp down our stairs and my husband has a piece of wood that he places the sleds behind, two at a time. He lifts the wood and then down the stairs they go! We have pillows at the end to catch the sleds so hopefully they won't crash and break, but we've always had to have a "Pit Stop", time for everyone to re-glue something that has fallen off! We run our races like a Pinewood Derby. We write down everyone's names on a bracket and they all get to race multiple times and it is so much fun to see who starts to pull ahead. One year Grandma and Grandpa won the whole thing and the teenagers could NOT believe it! I usually have prizes for 1st, 2nd and 3rd, and it's a fun night for everyone. It seems like whenever I tell anyone about this tradition, it becomes a new tradition in their family too. It is definitely an activity that everyone will enjoy and remember!

Debbie McEwen | www.madefrompinterest.com

For a few years when you were little a wonderful Santa Claus came to our home in December. He would ring his heavy, leather, bell clad strap at the front door...you would run to the door and in he would come with his pack on his back. He would gather you up and tell you a story, always about children who would help someone in need. He would tell you how you must be kind and good all year round, then he would have Dad and me sit on the sofa together and he would tell you how blessed you were to have a mom and dad who love you. Finally, he would take candy canes from his pack and pass them around. Then he would tell you that he was going to go out and get into his sleigh and go visit other children. He would tell you to run to the back window and look up in the sky and look for the little red light and wave good-bye to him and the reindeer.

(Santa was a sweet brother who went to church with us, and who visited lots of children each year. I loved having him come because he was a spiritual Santa. He was such a good Santa that even your dad never could guess who he was. When we moved away I finally told him and he was amazed because he actually was a young father.)

The Badger Family | Utah (written by my mother)

WINTER

ALL ABOUT ME: AN ANNUAL INTERVIEW

I take a lot of pictures of my kids. I always have a camera with me and my kids know that no matter the occasion, no matter where we go, pictures are going to happen. But what I love just as much as photos are their little words: the funny things they say including what they think about and how they view the world. Years ago, I started doing an annual interview with my kids and it's seriously my favorite thing EVER. At first it was only on paper, but now I do video too. The end of each year is a great time to do the interviews, and it's a fun tradition to have over the holiday and new year season.

I like to ask the same questions from year-to-year because the comparison is just too fun. Occasionally I will add new questions and then they'll stay on the list for every year after that. Personally, I don't like to use too many questions because my kids start to lose interest after awhile—especially the younger ones. Follow-up questions are the best though because depending on what you ask, you'll get some of the funniest and most endearing answers . . .

. . . . . .

KATE, AGE 4

Are you going to get married?

Yes, but I'm not going to kiss a boy on the lips. I am not doing that. I will kiss him on the cheek.

What's going to be your job when you grow up?

Mopping the floor and cleaning the kitchen.

Anything else?

I'm going to be a girl doctor.

How many kids are you going to have?

Five.

What will their names be?

Lily.

All of them? Yes.

EMMA, AGE 6

What's your job going to be when you grow up?

Can I be a Mom? Yeah, I pick that one. But I still know 2+2. No matter what, I know what 2+2 is.

What's your favorite thing about yourself?

That I can read, and I'm smart. I know what lots of things equal. And I have pretty hair.

HENRY, AGE 4

Will you have kids when you grow up?

Yep, 90 kids.

Are you going to get married?

No way.

Who is going to take care of the kids?

You are, Mom.

These interviews are absolute treasures and every time I read through them, I find myself smiling, laughing, and even tearing up a little bit. These kids of ours change so quickly and although it doesn't seem like it on a daily basis, looking back it's easy to see how much growth they've experienced over a year's time. My kids love hearing the interviews too and we all smile, laugh, and reminisce. I love every age my kids pass through, but I also love holding on to little pieces of each one along the way.

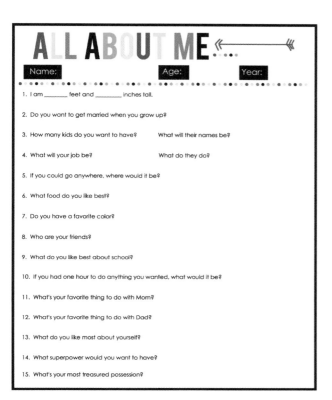

I created a fun questionnaire that you can print and use. Just copy and paste the following link into your computer's address bar then save to your computer and print!

The first week of the New Year we sit down as a family and set individual and family goals for the year. We print them out and leave them up all year in a place we look at often (inside our pantry door). As we pass off a goal, we can put a check mark by it. At the start of the next year, we always put the old goals in a binder all together. The kids love to look back to previous years when they had goals like, move to a big girl bed, or, learn to sing my ABC's.

The Carn Family

FIRST DAY OF SNOW DOUGHNUTS

How a southern Utah girl came to love snow I'm not sure. Growing up in a warm climate means no snow, and no real understanding of exactly how cold it actually gets. I remember going shopping in preparation for our move to the northern most part of Utah after our wedding and buying a thin jacket—I can't even call it a coat—and thinking it would be sufficient for a cold, snowy winter. I had no idea what I was in for! Don't laugh, but we only made in six months! We changed schools and moved a little south to the Salt Lake area to attend the university there where it was *slightly* warmer. Two years later we moved to Michigan and my love for the snow and the four seasons was sealed.

Now I love snow and so do my kids. We love everything that comes with it—building snowmen, tobogganing, sledding, cross country skiing, playing in the snow for hours, building snow caves, and then coming in for hot chocolate.

There's nothing more beautiful than the first snow, and our family loves to kick off the winter season by having doughnuts. We all look forward to those first flakes of snow coming down! We lived in Texas for two years and since we didn't get any snow there, we just decided to celebrate on the first day of winter.

Depending on when the first day of winter falls, we either buy doughnuts from our favorite bakery or we make our own. These yummy doughnuts couldn't be easier to make and they are absolutely delicious! You can do any kind of toppings you like—powdered sugar, cinnamon and sugar, glaze, or chocolate with sprinkles—on one, or all!

Doughnuts, hot chocolate, a cozy fire, and snow . . . perfection!

· · · · · ·

SNOWFLAKE DOUGHNUTS

INGREDIENTS

Flaky Grand Biscuits
cinnamon & sugar
powdered sugar
vegetable oil

♥ Pop open the biscuits can and lay out the dough on a piece of wax paper. Use a small round cookie cutter or biscuit cutter to remove the center of the biscuit. Place both pieces (the "hole" and the doughnut) back on the wax paper, and repeat until all of them are cut out.

♥ Pour oil in your skillet (I usually do about an inch or so. You don't need a lot!). Let it heat up to about 350 degrees. Oil can be tricky—if it's too hot, the outside will burn or get brown quickly while the inside will be doughy. If it's not hot enough, the dough will soak up too much oil and be super greasy. Once it's at 350 degrees, I would do a test run—just to make sure your oil is set—and before you put all your dough in!

♥ Add your dough hearts to the oil, and let one side turn golden brown, and then use tongs to turn them over to the other side.

♥ As soon as each heart is golden brown on each side, remove from the skillet and immediately place in a bowl of either powdered sugar or cinnamon and sugar. I prep bowls ahead of time so I just plop it in and use a spoon to make sure it's covered.

♥ Place on a plate covered with a paper towel and let rest until ready to eat. I don't think you'll have to wait long . . . these will be gobbled up fast!

LOVE BUCKETS

As parents, we're always looking for ways to strengthen the relationships that we have with our kids and that they have with each other. Let's be real—sometimes kids argue and they don't always get along. Ours are no different. Despite that, they do love each other and giving them ways to express that love has been key in our family.

Several years ago I was looking for a way to celebrate our family during the Valentine holiday and Love Buckets came to be. I found cute metal buckets—one for each person—cut hearts out of scrapbook paper and cardstock, then set out pencils and crayons.

Beginning February 1st, we write love notes to each member of the family every day, and place them in the buckets. Little ones that can't write yet draw pictures, and ask for help to spell words. I like to add a little candy in with my notes! We keep our Love Buckets out on a counter or shelf, and excitement builds every day as they can see the piles of notes grow and even bulge out of the pails.

On Valentine's Day, after our special dinner, we all sit down together and look through our pails. I liken the revealing of the love buckets to Christmas morning—their little cheeks brighten with anticipation, and big grins tug across their faces as they read what their siblings and parents wrote about them. The feeling in the air is indescribable; it becomes an extra special time.

It's a very simple yet meaningful way to share appreciation and love for each other and it's most definitely one of my favorite traditions of all.

• • • • • •

DETAILS

♥ Check for pails at your local hobby or craft store, or even the dollar store. If you start looking around Valentine's Day, you should be able to find them in red, pink, and white. The metal ones are really cute too!

♥ Add names or initials to your buckets so everyone knows whose they are!

♥ Add vinyl lettering or write directly on the bucket.

♥ Print your kids' names or initials on white cardstock (cute alphabet stickers work well too!), cut out into a rectangle or square shape (or use a circle punch for a circle), then mat onto a cute piece of scrapbook paper. Punch a hole in the top, and use ribbon or twine to attach to the handle of the pail.

OTHER LOVE IDEAS

♥ Create a Valentine tree! Gather branches from around your backyard and place them in a pitcher. Cut out hearts from colored paper, punch holes in the top, then set them out with pens or markers. Write love notes on the hearts, then hang them on the tree!

♥ Make a love rug! My sister's family uses one and loves it. They have one member of the family sit on the Valentines rug and while sitting there, everyone goes around and says something they love about that person. They take turns expressing and receiving these sweet sentiments and its a definite uplift for the whole family!

♥ Decorate bedroom doors with hearts! Cut out a bunch of hearts in all sizes, and then each night, place a heart on each child's bedroom with something you love written on it. If more than one child is in the room, just write names at the top of the hearts. Other members of the family can add them too!

VALENTINE HEART BUNTING COUNTDOWN

I love holiday countdowns. I love them for so many reasons, including the fact that it really fosters an enthusiasm for whatever holiday we're celebrating. But holiday countdowns also encourage and support family togetherness. With all the "busyness" of life, it helps us to focus on our family and carve out time together that can so easily be eaten up by other things. Plus, it's just FUN!

Valentine's Day is the perfect time to celebrate as a family. I made a cute bunting with fourteen hearts and placed a Valentine activity on the back of each one.

Beginning on February 1st we do a Valentine activity each day! My motto is always simplicity so most of the things we do are easy crafts or projects that are doable in an hour—or more if we want to.

Another fun and easy way to do a countdown is by making a paper chain: Cut out fourteen strips of red and pink paper, write a Valentine activity on each one, then use a little glue or double stick tape to loop them together and make a chain. Hang it up where you can see it and take one off for each day!

. . . . . .

HOW TO MAKE A HEART BUNTING COUNTDOWN

♥ Cut 14 hearts out of red, pink, and white cardstock—or whatever colors you like! I made mine about 5 inches in diameter. You can decorate them however you like—add numbers if you want to count down using specific hearts.

♥ Write a Valentine activity on the back of each heart.

♥ Punch two holes at the top of each heart then string them on baker's twine. Another option: A few years ago I painted 14 tiny clothespins (I found them at my local craft/hobby store.). I then used them to clip the hearts onto a long piece of twine, string, or ribbon.

♥ Hang along a mantel or shelf, down a banister, on the front of a table, or across a large window or door.

I'm also sharing a printable that includes 14 activities that you can print out on Avery 8160 address labels—just stick them on the back! Enter the following URL address into the address bar of your internet browser, save, and print.

bit.ly/2aHoGIU

Wear red or pink day

Make homemade Valentines

Read a Valentine story

Read a Valentine story

Play Valentine Bingo

Make & decorate sugar cookies

Make & send special Valentines to grandparents

Cut out heart snowflakes

Make pink hot chocolate

Decorate doors with paper hearts

Make a Valentine paper chain

Have a pink tea party

"attack" a or neighbor

VALENTINE ACTIVITY IDEAS

♥ Valentine Bingo: This is fun to play with the little ones during the day before the school kids get home or as a Sunday afternoon activity. I like to use Valentine M&Ms as the markers!

To download a fun Valentine Bingo game, enter the following URL into your address bar. Scroll to the bottom of the post, then click on the links for the bingo cards to download and save to your computer. Print onto white cardstock!

bit.ly/2aAOSn1

♥ "Heart attack" friends/neighbors: Cut out hearts of all sizes and quietly put them on someone's garage door, front door, sidewalk, etc. Leave a plate of treats, then ring the bell and run!

♥ Make and decorate Valentine cookies: You can make your own cookies from scratch or use a sugar cookie mix. My favorite mix is by Betty Crocker—I always get asked for the recipe! My favorite gluten free sugar cookie mix is by Cherry-brook Kitchen. I make red, pink, and white frosting then let the kids go to town with sprinkles and decorating!

♥ Make heart snowflakes: Cut hearts out of red, pink, and white cardstock in different sizes and make snowflakes. It's fun to hang them with string or baker's twine from the mantel, light fixture, doorway, or window.

♥ Read a Valentine story: I head to the library the last week of January and stock up on Valentine's Day books. I'll put aside a couple for the countdown and set out the others for everyone to enjoy at any time.

♥ Watch a fun Valentine show: We love family movie nights so why not incorporate them into our countdown? I've included a list of our 14 favorite Valentine's Day movies for families!

♥ Make pink hot chocolate: This is such a favorite with my kids! Our family loves hot chocolate and making it pink is fun and festive. You can find the recipe on page 122.

♥ Make a Valentine chain with red, pink and white cardstock: If you're not using a chain as the countdown itself, it's always fun to make them really long and string along windows, doorways, or the mantel.

♥ Cut hearts out of paper and decorate the doors in your house: Smothering doors in pink, red, and white hearts just makes the whole house feel the love!

♥ Create Valentines for grandparents and other family: Making homemade Valentines for the people you love is always a fun tradition to have, especially for those that live far away. Set out cardstock, glitter, glue, paper doilies, pipe cleaner, any other embellishments you want, and let the kids go for it!

♥ Have a pink tea party: Pink hot chocolate and sandwiches cut into hearts. Have your kids invite their stuffed animals and baby dolls, and you've got all the makings of a perfectly pink tea party.

♥ Wear red and pink all day: This is so fun, especially for my school-aged kids. They love it when I do it too!

FAVORITE VALENTINE'S DAY MOVIES

I have loved passing on some of my favorite childhood movies to my own children and so many of these oldies are on this list! *Parent Trap, The Love Bug, Summer Magic, The Happiest Millionaire* . . . they bring back so many memories. Whether you have big kids or little kids, they're sure to make for an evening of Valentine fun!

• • • • • •

Most of these movies are rated G, and a few are rated PG. Common Sense Media is a resource that I've used to check movies for more rating information to find out about a movie before showing it to my kids.

♥ **The Love Bug, rated G**

The original version is definitely my favorite. I have loved it since I was little!

♥ **The Parent Trap, rated G**

Okay, this is probably one of my favorite movies of all time! Once again, I prefer the original version—I just love Maureen O'Hara, and Hayley Mills is adorable. I think I actually have parts of it memorized.

♥ **Lady and the Tramp, rated G**

That spaghetti scene? Yep—one of the sweetest Disney movie moments ever!

♥ **In the Good Old Summertime, unrated**

Judy Garland stars in this fun musical. It's charming the whole way through!

♥ **The Happiest Millionaire, rated G**

We always called this the "alligator" movie. Curious now? It stars Fred MacMurray, and it's SO MUCH FUN!

♥ **Enchanted, rated PG**

Modern day meets fairy tale . . .

♥ **The Princess Bride, rated PG**

Is there anything I really need to say about this movie?

♥ **Up, rated PG**

I just love this movie and I think it's one of the sweetest love stories. In fact, I cry everytime I watch it.

♥ **The Wizard of Oz, rated PG**

The Tin Man searching for a heart makes Valentine's Day a great time to watch this award-winning film and introduce it to your kids!

♥ **Summer Magic, rated G**

Hayley Mills stars in this Disney musical, and it's another one of my childhood favorites; an oldy, but a goody!

♥ **Wild Hearts Can't Be Broken, rated G**

This is a coming-of-age story, portraying a girl and her horse during the Great Depression. It sends the wonderful message of pursuing your dreams!

♥ **Beauty and the Beast, rated G**

Classic Disney cartoon and love story!

♥ **Alvin and The Chipmunks: The Valentines Collection, rated G**

I had to add this one in because my kids love Alvin and the Chipmunks cartoons! It's a fun, silly Valentine's movie!

♥ **Wall-E, rated G**

A curious and lovable robot falls in love!

14 DAYS OF VALENTINES

Our family has moved around a lot. In three short years we lived in three states and moved across the country twice. This meant a lot of changes in a short amount of time. We moved to upstate New York last year and I felt like doing something extra-special for my kids and husband to give them a little boost of joy. Valentine's Day was coming up so it seemed like the perfect time to do it. I created a 14 Days of Valentines plan that included a simple gift or treat to give my family members each day.

It was a huge hit and I can't tell you how wonderful it was to see them so excited about what they would find every morning. It had such an impact on our family and it was exactly what we needed at just the right time. We feel more settled in our new area now and are adjusting nicely to our lives here, but the 14 Days of Valentines has been added to our list of Valentine's Day traditions and it will definitely continue!

· · · · · ·

DETAILS

I gathered cute Valentine candy and some other treats and snacks I know my kids love, then made "cheesy" Valentine printables to go along with them . . . 14 in all! Starting February 1st they had a fun surprise every day for 14 days until Valentine's Day!

HERE ARE THE ITEMS I USED

♥ 1. Gummi Bears
(You are loved beary much)

♥ 2. York Peppermint Patties
(We were mint for each other)

♥ 3. Starburst
(You're a star)

♥ 4. Mini boxes of cereal
(I cereal-sly love you)

♥ 5. Swedish Fish
(You are o"fish"ally my valentine)

♥ 6. Blow Pops
(You blow me away)

♥ 7. Hershey Hugs & Kisses
(Hugs & Kisses)

♥ 8. Peanut M&M's
(I love you More & More)

♥ 9. Reese's Pieces
(I love you to pieces)

♥ 10. Mini Popcorn Bags
(You make my heart pop)

♥ 11. Bag of chips
(You're all that and a bag of chips)

♥ 12. Pop Rocks (You rock)

♥ 13. Flavored Milk Straws
(You are ex-straw-ordinary)

♥ 14. Sweetheart Conversation Hearts
(You are sweet)

Some of the items I bought were in individual boxes or pieces (like the Reese Pieces, Pop Rocks, Conversation Hearts, etc.). It ended up being less expensive that way for certain candies. But I bought most of the candies in bags or in bulk and then divided them up. I used snack bags to portion them out, added the printable label, then placed all the snack bags for that item in a large gallon bag. In the end I had 13 large gallon bags and one larger bag for the cereal. That way I could grab one each night and they were totally ready to go. The gallon bags went right back in my pantry since they were still clean!

I put the candy bags on my kids' kitchen stools each night so they'd be sure to find them at breakfast. You can gift them in the morning, put them in the kids' lunches, or even have them after dinner—whatever works the best for you.

To print the labels, enter the URL below into the address bar of your computer. Save to your computer, and then print onto Avery Address Labels 8160.

bit.ly/2b9KMGM

GIVING DADDY'S CAR A HEART ATTACK

As a CPA for a large accounting firm, every year January to March is an exceptionally time busy for my husband, known to us as "busy season." It meant that we wouldn't really see him for the duration of that time, especially the kids, who were very young. They were asleep when he left in the morning, and asleep when he came home at night, so we had to think outside the box in order to find ways to see him during those long weeks.

Valentine's Day fell during that time period, and while we were doing most of our celebrating, my husband needed to be at work. We included him however possible, but he missed a lot, and we missed him.

One year I got an idea, and the kids were SO excited about it, they could hardly stand it. Trying to get kids four years old and under to keep a secret is quite the feat! For Family Night the week of Valentine's Day, we cut out as many hearts as we could out of red, pink, and white cardstock. I got out markers and crayons, and any little embellishments I had lying around, and they worked hard creating a bunch of Valentines for their dad.

When they finished, I bundled all the kids up, piled them in the car, and drove to where my husband parked his car at work. We quickly got to work decorating his car, covering it in hearts from bumper to fender. I got the windows and top of the hood, and wherever the kids couldn't reach. We also unlocked the car, and left a few treats and more hearts on his seat. Once the "heart attacking" was complete, we drove home, singing songs and feeling so happy about what we had done. The kids could not stop talking about their dad, and when he might find the hearts, and what he would say. The pinnacle came when he came home, and woke the kids up to hug them and kiss them, and tell them that he loved all their hearts. What a sweet, tender moment—it sealed our new tradition, and we have loved it every year since.

If there's someone you love, whether you see them all the time or not very often, giving their car (or place where they live) a heart attack is a simple, fun, and heartfelt way to reach out and let them know how much you love and appreciate them!

. . . . . .

♥ Let your kids make the hearts as much as they can, depending on their age and ability. My favorite hearts are the ones that are lopsided, crooked, and have a pint of glue on them! I taught my kids how to cut out a heart by folding a piece of paper in half, and cutting out one side of the heart. Even my five year olds wanted to try!

♥ Our favorite embellishments are crayons and markers, but occasionally I'll pull out any extra craft supplies I have, like glitter, Styrofoam stickers or regular stickers, and washi tape.

♥ When heart attacking a car, make sure you use a tape that's safe for them. We use painters' tape—it comes off very easily and doesn't scratch the paint.

PINK HOT CHOCOLATE

I had no idea what a hit this would be the first time I made it for my kids, but it was an instant success. It debuted at our Valentine's Day breakfast a couple of years ago, and they loved it so much, it's now part of our annual Valentine's Day Countdown. It's one of the yummiest traditions around!

It's such a simple recipe, and can be made in less than 10 minutes, which I love. It's easy to whip up a batch on Valentine's Day morning, or any other time you want to make it. When serving, I give my kids the choice of whipped cream or marshmallows, and then Valentine sprinkles for the top. They love creating their own special drink, and it makes it even more fun!

· · · · · ·

INGREDIENTS

3–4 cups milk
1 can evaporated milk
12 oz. pkg. white
　　chocolate chips
red food coloring

DIRECTIONS

♥ In a saucepan over low heat, melt the white chocolate chips with the evaporated milk.

♥ Once melted, add the whole milk and heat through. Start with 3 cups, and add more to taste.

♥ Remove from heat, and add drops of red food coloring until you get it to the color you like.

♥ Serve with whipped cream or marshmallows, plus a few fun sprinkles for the top!

A few days before Valentine's Day, we draw names and everyone has to MAKE a Valentine for the person whose name they drew. We keep it all a secret and then on Valentine's Day we slip the Valentine onto the dinner plate of the person we have when no one is looking. It is all very ceremonious, so you can't look at your Valentine until it's your turn. We usually start with the youngest person looking at theirs, then the person they got the Valentine from gets to look at theirs, etc. We have done this for many years, and it is a sweet thing.

The Pennock Family | Idaho

HEART-SHAPED MEAL IDEAS

I don't know what it is about hearts, but they make everything more fun! One of my favorite things to do for my kids on Valentine's Day is to make fun heart-shaped meals.

A heart cookie cutter is my main tool, and I like to use it on everything I can get my hands on! For preschool snacks or a snack for school lunches, I love to send heart-shaped cheese with crackers. So cute, and the kids love it!

For lunch, I use the cookie cutter on peanut butter sandwiches, then add a side of "x's and o's", which are slices of cucumber or grapes with baby carrots placed in an x. When I can find it, I like to buy Strawberry Crush, but when I can't, a bottle of milk with a cute striped straw is adorable too!

Dinner brings heart-shaped pizza—my trusty heart cookie cutter works well on refrigerated biscuits—then the kids can add whatever topping they like.

I mostly love simple ways to turn a regular meal into an extra-special one. It makes me so happy to see my kids so excited, and a fun way to celebrate the holiday together.

. . . . . .

HERE ARE A FEW OTHER MEAL IDEAS

♥ Turn fruit kabobs into Cupid's arrows by adding a paper arrow tip and feathers

♥ One-eyed Jacks with a heart: Cut a heart out of the center of a piece of bread, butter it on both sides, then place on a hot griddle. Crack an egg into the center of the heart, and cook through on both sides.

♥ Heart-shaped French toast or pancakes are perfect for breakfast . . . or for dinner!

♥ Make a Valentine's Day trail mix, using pink and red M&M's plus craisins, nuts, Chex cereal, pretzels, and whatever you like!

♥ Homemade heart doughnuts make a fun treat: Use a heart cookie cutter to cut out refrigerated biscuit dough, then deep fry and sprinkle with powdered sugar or cinnamon and sugar.

♥ Make your favorite muffin or cupcake recipe, and fill the paper liners with batter as you normally would. Stick a marble on one side of the liner, so it created a heart shape, then bake as normal.

♥ Grilled cheese sandwiches in the shape of a heart are one of favorite lunch or even dinner ideas. Serve with tomato soup . . . it's red and perfect!

♥ Fruit, cheese slices, sandwiches, cookies—use a heart cookie cutter on just about anything to make it perfect for Valentine's Day!

RASPBERRY BROWNIE TORTE

Valentine's Day just wouldn't be complete without a decadent dessert for the ones you love, and chocolate is always a best bet! A couple of years ago I found a recipe for chocolate torte that looked fabulous, and I wanted to make it for my family for our Valentine's Day dinner, but I just wasn't going to have the time to make it. Instead, I created a brownie torte that was incredibly simple but looked and tasted like it took me all day! My husband loved it, my kids loved it, and I loved it. We were hooked, and now it's my go-to Valentine's Day dessert.

Layers of rich, chocolate-y brownie and fresh whipped cream, then balanced with the perfect tartness of raspberries create my Raspberry Brownie Torte. Divine. And SO easy! A torte usually refers to layers of cake, and you could certainly do that instead, but I'm a brownie lover, and I thought the extra gooey-ness of them would be fabulous . . . and it IS! It also meant that it would a lot easier and faster, which is what I love most of all!

• • • • • •

INGREDIENTS

1 brownie mix (that makes a 9 x 13 pan—I like Ghirardelli

1 pint heavy cream

½ cup powdered sugar

fresh raspberries

6 oz. pkg. chocolate chips

DIRECTIONS

♥ Make brownie mix according to package directions, or your favorite brownie recipe. Divide the batter evenly and bake in two separate baking dishes (or one larger dish), so the brownies will be thin. Make sure you alter the baking time so they don't burn or get crispy, since there's less batter in each baking dish. I actually used a gluten-free brownie mix for this batch, and since it called for an 8 x 8 pan, I used a 9 x 13 baking dish instead, and it worked perfectly!

♥ While the brownies are baking, whip heavy cream until soft peaks form.

♥ Add powdered sugar a couple of tablespoons at a time. Once the brownies have cooled, use a biscuit cutter to cut circles out of them! If you don't have them, you can always use a cookie cutter, or even a drinking glass.

♥ Starting with a brownie circle on the bottom of each serving plate, add a dollop of whipped cream and smooth to the edges of the brownie. Top with another brownie and more whipped cream. Repeat, and top with a few raspberries! Melt some chocolate chips or baking chocolate and drizzle over the top of the torte, and a little on the plate.

♥ The brownies bake faster because they're thinner, and everything else can be prepped when they're baking. You could even make the brownies the day or night before, then just quickly assemble before dinner or your party.

POPCORN LOLLIPOPS

Popped popcorn and gooey marshmallow are combined to form these delightful popcorn balls, and then they're topped with white chocolate and dipped in sprinkles. They're a huge hit with my kids, and they're really fun for every holiday, including Valentine's Day!

It's a great recipe for kids to get involved with—mine love covering their hands in butter so they can roll the popcorn balls, then doing the dipping, and especially adding the sprinkles. A lot of sprinkles.

They're perfect to make on a snow day or cold day (yes, we have those!) home from school, or during the day with the little ones not old enough for school. We also like to make them on a Sunday afternoon for our Sunday treat, or for Family Night during the month of February.

. . . . . .

INGREDIENTS

10 oz. pkg. mini
marshmallows
4 Tbsp. butter
16 cups popped popcorn
1 package white
chocolate chips
valentine sprinkles
lollipop/popsicle sticks

♥ Place the popped popcorn in an extra large bowl, with plenty of room to stir. Melt the butter in a large saucepan over medium high heat. Add the marshmallows, and stir constantly until smooth. Pour the marshmallow mixture over the popcorn, and use a wooden spoon to completely cover the popcorn.

♥ Let the mixture sit for about 5–10 minutes, to let the marshmallow cool—but not harden. Coat your hands with butter, then form the popcorn mixture into firm balls. Place them on a piece of wax paper that has also been rubbed with a little butter. (Don't use cooking spray—it leaves a yucky taste on the popcorn.)

♥ Once all the popcorn balls are formed, push the popsicle/sucker sticks into the center of each ball. I also like using paper straws! Melt the white chocolate chips in a glass bowl in the microwave. Start with 30 seconds, stir, then another 15–30 seconds and stir until smooth. Dip the top half of the popcorn balls into the white chocolate, then immediately add the sprinkles. Refrigerate until time to serve. Makes 6–8 popcorn balls, depending on size.

A VALENTINE MORNING SURPRISE

Our oldest son was born when we were very young, and still college undergraduates. We had many years left of being poor students, and didn't have money for many extras. I was so excited, and wanted to do really fun things for all the holidays, but it meant coming up with inexpensive ideas and ways to celebrate.

One Valentine's Day morning one year, I surprised my little boy with a cute heart balloon tied to his chair at the table, along with a little bag of candy. When he came down the stairs and into the kitchen and saw what had been left for him, squeals of excitement filled the air. It was a simple thing, and didn't cost a lot of money, but he loved it so much, and was completely thrilled.

I knew then and there that it was a tradition that would continue.

It's been awhile since that first balloon surprise. College degrees have been completed, and we've added five more children to our family, but I still put a Valentine balloon and bag of candy out at each child's plate to be found when they dash down the stairs on Valentine's Day morning. I wait until they're fast asleep on Valentine's Eve, and then I go to work, setting everything out, and getting the table set for breakfast.

It's so simple, and a small gesture, but one that fills our home with joy!

• • • • • •

♥ Check your local dollar store to see if they have helium balloons—I always look there first, and I've found that they have really reasonable prices, and usually a good selection! Our local grocery stores also have balloons for all the holidays.

♥ There are some really fun options for candy containers: takeout boxes, paper treat bags sealed with washi tape, mason jars, wrapped boxes, and clear plastic treat bags. All of these items can be found at your local craft or hobby store. I've used all of those things before, but I actually use sandwich bags a lot—I just use scissors to cut the Ziploc part off the top! I always have them on hand, so it makes it really easy and inexpensive.

♥ I fill the bags with candy, tie them shut with ribbon, and tie the balloon onto the bag. The candy holds the balloon in place, and they look so cute on the kitchen table! It's the decorations and the treat, all in one!

We have a "Family Bubble Wrap Stomp." Each person gets a piece of bubble wrap to jump on after we count down to midnight!

Thomas Family | Texas

We have a new tradition which is on Chinese New Year. We clean the house and buy clementines and fortune cookies. We eat Chinese food and read stories about the holiday, in honor of Avery, to celebrate her family history. The girls love to wear their dresses from China. This year we will be celebrating it with friends. It is also traditional to give out envelopes of money, "red envelopes", wishing people to be prosperous. Most parents give out silver dollars. We make lanterns and send a lantern off into the sky. It can also be celebrated with fireworks.

Rothermael Family | Georgia

When Jeff and I were dating, I started our family Valentine's Day tradition. I sneaked into his apartment and "heart attacked" his kitchen. On each heart I wrote all the things I loved about him, spending time to be sure they were meaningful. It was a labor of love, and I realized afterwards that was what made it extra special. Every year since then, our family has continued this tradition. We spend the Monday night before Valentine's Day writing on construction paper hearts what we love about each other. (Some years, as a surprise, I have also asked grandparents to write hearts!) I encourage the kids to take their time to think of something specific and meaningful, then we run to opposite sides of the house so no one can see what we write! When everyone has finished, I collect them all in a ziplock bag and hide them until Valentine's Day morning. After the kids are in bed the night before, I tape the hearts all over the kitchen -on the cabinets, on the fridge, and even on the walls. On Valentine's Day morning, the air is filled with warm, gooey cinnamon rolls, and, so much love and tenderness. I love watching the kids as they wake up and lumber into the kitchen, their eyes lighting up when they see the pink and red explosion, excited to read their hearts. I cry every year when I read the sweet and thoughtful things they write; there really is nothing that warms my heart more! My kids have taken their hearts afterwards to put in their special memory boxes, so I know this tradition is meaningful to them as well.

The Norman Family | Arizona

YOU'RE MY LUCKY CHARM

I remember the first time my mom gave us colored milk. She made blue for the boys and pink for the girls, and we sat there in awe of her magical abilities to turn something ordinary to something extraordinary. We begged her to tell us how she did it, but she just smiled, and told us that one day, when we were moms and dads, she would tell us the secret.

Now my kids ask me the same questions, and it's my turn to receive that same look of amazement when I hand them a glass of colored milk. Even my teenager, who knows the "secret recipe," enjoys being part of the fun.

One of my favorite times to make it for them is St. Patrick's Day, in a bright green color that's perfect for the occasion. Served with a bowl of magically delicious Lucky Charms, they consider it the best ever. We only have sugar cereal on special occasions, so it makes this breakfast even more exciting!

The best part is that it's a simple thing that takes just a few minutes to put together. A fun "You're My Lucky Charm" tag is the perfect touch! On St. Patrick's Day Eve, I'll set bowls of cereal (sans milk), and cute milk bottles or glasses with the tag tied around them. In the morning it's easy to add milk to their cereal, and whip up a batch of colored milk!

· · · · · ·

GREEN MILK RECIPE

INGREDIENTS

1 cup milk
2-3 drops green
     food coloring
a little sugar to taste

YOU'RE MY LUCKY CHARM PRINTABLE

Enter the following link in the address bar of your computer. Save the file to your computer, then print onto white cardstock. Cut out circles, punch a hole in the top, and attach to milk bottles.

bit.ly/2b1SB0N

SHAMROCK FLOATS

I love making floats, and they take me back to my own childhood. I remember having "purple cows," and how much we loved them! My kids now love them too, and they make an appearance on a fairly regular basis throughout the summer especially. There are so many fun options and ways to mix and match ice cream and soda that are perfect for the every day, but also for the holidays.

One of our favorite floats is the Shamrock Float, and it's the most delicious combination of mint chocolate chip ice cream and lemon-lime soda. They have become a tradition, and are now an important part of our St. Patrick's Day menu.

Floats are really fast and easy to make, whether you're serving just a few, or a crowd. I also love that they're so easy to customize for each person you're serving them to. Some of my kids love lots of ice cream and just a little bit of soda pop, and others love the soda best, with just a small scoop of ice cream. And . . . some of them just like one or the other!

If you're having a family party, or inviting friends over to celebrate this day of green, it's the perfect treat to serve!

INGREDIENTS

mint chocolate chip ice cream

lemon-lime soda

whipped cream

green sprinkles

DIRECTIONS

· Scoop ice cream into wide-mouth mason jars or large glasses.

· Pour desired amount of soda on top.

· Then add whipped cream and sprinkles!

We have a leprachaun named Lucky that visits us for St. Patrick's Day. He of course turns our milk green, and he always comes throughout the day and leaves gold candies (Rolos). The kids also like to make him little leprachaun houses. He's sneaky though, we've never seen him once. They also like to write notes to him and he is usually good about responding.

The Thomas Family | Texas

EASTER BASKET TREASURE HUNT

From the time our oldest son was little, we decided that we would have the Easter Bunny come to our house on Saturday, and it has been that way ever since. It allows us to do all the fun things that day, and then focus on the spiritual aspect of the holiday on Easter Sunday, when we attend church and celebrate the reason for Easter, our Savior, Jesus Christ. It's really worked for our family, and we love the balance that it gives.

Another benefit is that we have plenty of time on Saturday for so many of our fun traditions, including our annual Easter Basket Treasure Hunt! How the kids love following clues—reading them and trying to figure out the next one, all while picturing what could possibly be at the very end of the hunt.

We've used everything from simple yellow Post-its to fun, printable clues, but no matter which way we do it, it's so much fun.

We start by giving them the first clue, and depending on their ages, make it more or less difficult. They continue to search for and find each clue after that, until it ultimately leads to their baskets' hiding place. Our kids absolutely love it! Another variation is to leave a little prize at each clue—like some candy, or something from their basket.

If you have older kids, you can either do a separate hunt for them with more difficult clues, or have them help create the clues for the younger children. This is definitely an activity that the whole family can be involved in. With a large age gap in our kids' ages, this has been important for our family, and our oldest son enjoys being involved in creating the hunt for his siblings

· · · · · ·

I've included some really fun fill-in-the-blank printable clues that you can use for your own Easter Basket Treasure Hunt! Print onto white cardstock, cut them out, then fill in the blanks with your clues!

bit.ly/2aWDsLc

EASTER BASKET IDEAS

- Tin pails

- Paint cans (new—you can find them at Home Depot or Lowe's, etc.)

- Apple baskets

- Canvas totes (embellish them, or let your kids decorate them!)

WHAT DOES THE EASTER BUNNY LEAVE IN OUR BASKETS?

He loves to leave things for the upcoming seasons—spring and summer. After a long winter, we're always excited about getting out and enjoying the sun! Here are a few of the things we've done in the past:

- Summer stuff! Sunglasses, flip flops, sand toys, etc.

- Bubbles and sidewalk chalk

- Candy, of course!

- Art supplies

- Matchbox cars

- Books

- Outside games or toys

- Chapstick/ Lip gloss for the girls

- Nail polish

- New hair bows/headbands

YOU'VE BEEN EGG'ED!

Imagine a carful of kids, hands moving rapidly, and voices talking with excitement as exit strategies are analyzed, and plans are carefully made. Should they try and run back to the car? Or hide in the bushes next to the house? Who gets to leave the treats? Who gets to tuck in the note? And most importantly, whose turn is it to ring the doorbell?

Leaving treats anonymously at the doorsteps of our friends and neighbors is one of my kids' very favorite things to do, and a holiday just gives us even more of an excuse! Some of my favorite memories include our crazy attempts at delivering cookies, and me waiting in the truck with the lights dimmed until I hear peals of laughter getting louder and louder heading my way. I relish my part as the getaway driver, and I think I'm pretty good at it!

This is the spring version of "You've Been Boo'ed," and it's such a great activity for families of all ages—everyone loves it, from the littles, up through to the teenagers, as well as the adults!

As parents, we are always looking for ways to teach our children about serving others—to think of other people, what they might need, and how we can help. Yes, dropping treats off and trying to escape without being seen is really fun, but it also incorporates turning our thoughts to others. Whether it's an older widow or widower, someone who has just had surgery or suffered a loss, or a family that we just can't get out of our minds, it's a wonderful way to spread some cheer and brighten a day. The way it makes our children (and us) feel is undeniable, and the fact that it makes us all roll on the floor with laughter is an extra-added benefit.

· · · · · ·

DETAILS

Save your egg cartons (I like cardboard ones the best!), and let your kids decorate them. This is just one more part that they can be involved in, and adds to the whole experience. Fill plastic eggs with Easter candy, and then place them in the empty carton. You can also use a cute pail or basket, fill with plastic or paper grass, and then set your eggs on top. Another cute version would be to decorate sugar cookies in the shape of Easter eggs and use those! Tie with ribbon and add the cute tag and instructions, and you're ready for delivery! The instructions include information on how to pass it along to the next person, so it ends up being a chain effect—spreading throughout a neighborhood and community.

Decide who you want to deliver them to, and then under the guise of night, ring the doorbell, leave the eggs, and run! Get ready for a night of fun, laughter, and memories that will add to your list of treasured Easter traditions.

I've created a darling printable for you that includes a tag and all the instructions for you and the person you're delivering them too. Enjoy!

Enter the link below into your browser. Download and save to your computer. Print on white cardstock!

bit.ly/2b9KKhY

MAILING PLASTIC EASTER EGGS

A couple of years ago around Eastertime, I was expecting our sixth baby. I was due just a week after Easter, and as the holiday approached, I was finding I had less and less energy to do many of our normal holiday activities. I wanted to come up with something fun I could do for the kids that would be relatively easy for me to do, and so I decided to send my kids a fun surprise through the mail . . . Easter Eggs filled with candy!

I was like a kid waiting for Christmas morning—I couldn't wait for them to come! When they did finally arrive, it was utterly delightful to see the kids' faces when they opened the door and found five plastic Easter eggs on the front porch, addressed to them! There were squeals of delight and surprise as they opened them up and found their favorite Easter candy inside, and I knew from that moment a tradition was born.

If you have children, grandchildren, or other loved ones you'd like to send a special Easter surprise too, this is the perfect thing! You could also include stickers and other small gifts instead of or in addition to candy. Themed eggs would also be fun!

DIRECTIONS

· Remove the lids from the eggs and fill the bottoms with Easter grass, tissue paper, or other filler. I knew that my candy weighed quite a bit, so I used a little more grass.

· Add desired candy, stickers, and other items, then put the lids back on.

· Write or print addresses on address labels (make sure you get ones that will fit on the size of egg you chose!), and center them on the tops of your eggs.

· Use clear packing tape all around the egg to keep it closed in transit, and protect the address labels.

· Head to your local post office and mail! If your eggs are light enough, and you have enough stamps, you can also just add the appropriate postage and put in your mail box (if they'll fit!) or a blue postal box.

SUPPLIES

large plastic Easter eggs
easter grass or other filler such as tissue paper
easter candy
stickers or other small gifts
address labels
clear packing tape

· You can really any size egg you like, but keep in mind you'll need to fit an address on there!

· I like the large eggs with a clear lid—it's fun to be able to see inside!

· I've found the eggs at my local dollar store, Joann Fabrics, Michaels Arts & Crafts, and Hobby Lobby.

CONFETTI EGGS

Ginger Bowie, gingersnapcrafts.com

My grandmother started the tradition of having confetti eggs at Easter when I was a kid. She would hold huge Easter egg hunts with hundreds of eggs for all of the grandchildren. We would look forward to these every year! She would make each grandchild a confetti egg with their name on it. She would hide the confetti eggs along with the rest of the Easter eggs. If we found our own egg we would get a dollar. Yes, a whole dollar! If we found someone else's egg we would run and bop them on the head. We would have confetti everywhere: in our hair, on our clothes and in the yard. We had a blast chasing each other around with those eggs!

We have continued that tradition with our kids, and they love it just as much.

You can make you own confetti eggs like my grandmother did!

SUPPLIES

an egg for each person in your family

large needle or something pokey

egg dye (vinegar and water)

confetti

tissue paper

1-inch circle punch

school glue

vinyl lettering (optional)

DIRECTIONS

- You'll begin by gently tapping the end of an egg with a sharp object. A huge sewing needle or corn-on- the-cob poker both do a great job.

- Once you have a good size hole you can empty the egg yolk into a bowl. Rinse your eggs out and let dry.

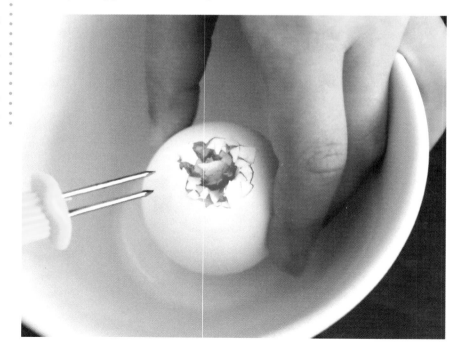

- In the meantime mix your egg dye with vinegar and water according to the package directions.

- Dye your eggs as you normally do.

- Let the eggs dry completely.

- To make the confetti I have my kiddos punch a ton of colorful circles with hole punchers. You can also buy confetti at your local party store.

- Use a 1-inch circle punch to cut out some colorful circles using tissue paper. Once your eggs are dry and filled with confetti, use school glue to glue the tissue paper circles around the openings. Let dry.

- I use vinyl lettering to label each egg with our names. You can always use a Sharpie like my grandmother did! That works just as well! Now the only thing left to do is hide some eggs, and then bop someone on the head!

- Some years I buy the confetti eggs in the store, but I find that when I take the time like my grandmother did to make each family member a handmade confetti Easter egg, it makes this tradition that much better. I can imagine my grandmother taking the time to make our eggs. It really makes me feel close to her. I am grateful for my grandmother and the many family traditions that started with her and still continue today through my siblings and cousins

RESURRECTION ROLLS

Easter is a delightful holiday, full of dyed eggs, candy, egg hunts, yummy food, and even the Easter bunny. Our family absolutely loves Eastertime, and it's always a wonderful two weeks of traditions.

Amidst all the jelly beans and Easter eggs, we especially want our children to know and understand the real reason we celebrate it, why it's a holiday, and how it's special. We don't want all the fun parts to overshadow what is most important, which is the resurrection of our Savior, Jesus Christ.

Resurrection rolls are an excellent way to teach children about the resurrection. They are incredibly easy to make, but the message is powerful and visual. Even the smallest child can be impacted by this simple activity, which makes it so wonderful for families of all ages.

The rolls start with a marshmallow in the middle, which melts as it bakes. When they're done, the centers are hollow, which represent the tomb of Jesus on Easter morning. When you break them open, they're empty! It's such a wonderful lesson, and it's something that can be done year after year.

The recipe is simple, and it's perfect for little hands to help with. Kids love dipping the marshmallows in butter, rolling them in the sugar, and then folding up the rolls. There's a job for everyone! As you're making the rolls, read the story of the resurrection from the Bible, which you can find in John 19–20, Luke 23–24, Matthew 27–28, or Mark 15–16. You can explain that the marshmallow represents Jesus and the roll is his tomb, adding in other details as you go.

I love activities that are hands-on, and then have a purpose or teach a lesson. These fit the bill in all cases, and they combine fun and meaningful.

· · · · · ·

INGREDIENTS

1 can refrigerated
crescent rolls
8 large marshmallows
6 Tbsp. melted butter
cinnamon and sugar

DIRECTIONS

· Preheat oven to 375 degrees. Start with a can of refrigerated crescent rolls, and separate them into individual triangles.

· Roll a large marshmallow into melted butter, then into cinnamon and sugar, then place it into the center one of the triangles.

· Roll it up, sealing all the edges really well with your fingers, so the marshmallow doesn't escape. Brush with melted butter.

· Place on a cookie sheet that's been sprayed with cooking spray, and bake for 12–15 minutes, or until done. You can also place them in a muffin tin that's been sprayed with cooking spray.

EASTER ADVENT

There are so many really fun things about Easter, including egg hunts, Easter baskets, colored eggs and yummy treats. We love all of those things, and they are most definitely a part of our holiday celebration. In our home, the true meaning of Easter lies with our Savior, Jesus Christ, and we want to teach our children and help them to acquire a deeper understanding of one of our most special holidays.

My kids love countdowns, so I created a weeklong Easter Advent to make it something they could look forward to each day.

It consists of eight different activities, with the first one starting on Palm Sunday. Most of them can be done on any day that you choose—there are just a couple activities that are meant to be on a specific day. If your house is like our house, weekdays are very busy, so I love that these are simple ideas that can fit into your regular routine.

It's such a wonderful way to lead up to Easter Sunday, spend time together as a family, and learn what Easter really means.

· · · · · ·

ADVENT ACTIVITIES

DAY 1 (PALM SUNDAY)

Make palms or hearts and write what you love about Jesus, and what He has done for you.

Cut leaves out of green construction paper, and cut fringes on the sides to make them look like palms. (You can also cut out hearts, if you would rather do that instead.) Write on each palm something that Christ has done for you, a characteristic He has that you would like to emulate, or something you love about Him. You can either pass out the palms so each family member can do a few of their own, or do each one as a family. This will probably depend a lot on the ages in your family. Hang the palms where you can see them, and be reminded throughout the week of what you wrote.

DAY 2

Read the Easter story in the Bible (Scripture Egg Hunt).

In addition to reading the story straight through, there is a scripture egg hunt that helps younger children visually connect with the story, although it's great for all ages. Details can be found online if you search "Easter Scripture Egg Hunt," and several different sites will give you all the info. You fill 12 eggs with everyday items that represent a part of the Easter story, and then go through them one-by-one, reading the scripture and talking about what happened.

DAY 3

Make Easter treats and share them with someone.

This activity is definitely a family favorite, because they all get to eat the treats too! They also love secretly delivering them to people, and it's a fun-filled night of service, laughter, and family togetherness.

DAY 4

Read an Easter book.

We love books at our house, and I always like to incorporate them into our countdowns. There aren't as many Easter books (religious) out there as compared to Christmas, so it might take a little more looking, but there are some good ones. I love story time with my kids, and even more so when a great conversation comes out of it.

DAY 5

Make a list (write or color) of things you want to work on and improve.

Easter is a time of thankfulness and rejoicing, and also hopefully a time of self-reflection. I can't think of a better time to sit down and write some goals of things you want to work on—taking Christ's example and trying to incorporate it into our own lives. Even the little ones can participate, and draw a picture of something they want to do better.

DAY 6

Do a secret act of service.

Is there an elderly neighbor that needs their walk shoveled? Or perhaps a family is in need of a meal or clothing? Maybe it's not so secret . . . visiting a local nursing home and taking time to talk to the residents or play music for them is a wonderful way to spread some cheer and do some service.

You could even make the goal as a family to do as many acts of service as possible during the day—holding doors open, smiling and giving compliments, looking for ways to help others—there are many small ways to serve!

DAY 7

Bake Resurrection Rolls.

I love the visual effect these yummy rolls provide—it's really a wonderful, hands-on activity for kids. They're easy to make, and perfect for a weekend breakfast or treat.

DAY 8

Easter Sunday Sunrise Breakfast.

Depending on where you live, and which month Easter falls in, it may be too cold to actually go outside. But whether you're inside or outside, rising early as a family to eat breakfast, watch the sun rise, and read about the resurrection is a magnificent way to celebrate Easter.

HOW TO PUT YOUR ADVENT TOGETHER

· Use a Sharpie to write numbers 1–8 on plastic Easter eggs, but you can also use stickers or vinyl numbers.

· Thread baker's twine (or other thin twine) through the already existing holes at the tops of the eggs. I did use a drill to make the holes a little bigger, but you could also use a needle to help you get the twine through if necessary.

· Print the advent activities onto white cardstock, then cut them into strips and place inside the eggs.

· I created my eggs to hang on branches, so it could double as Easter décor, and serve as a centerpiece for our kitchen table. I found a metal bucket at my local craft store, placed some floral foam in the bottom of the bucket, and then poked in branches we found in our yard.

SOME OTHER IDEAS FOR DISPLAYING YOUR ADVENT EGGS

· Thread your baker's twine as described, then . . .

· Use washi tape to hang each egg from your mantel (varying lengths would be cute!)

· Attach a piece of ribbon or jute along your mantel, then use clothespins to hang the eggs

· Use clothespins to clip them to a chicken wire frame

· Staple a piece of jute across the back of an empty frame, and use clothespins to clip the eggs (with baker's twine through the holes) across the jute. Place the frame on a mantel, shelf, or table, or even on an easel in your kitchen

Or, if you don't want to hang them, you can . . .
· Fill a tin pail or basket with Easter grass, and place your eggs on top

· Keep them inside a cardboard egg container, and decorate the top

DOWNLOAD PRINTABLE

Enter the following URL into your computer's address bar, and it will take you to the downloadable file. Save it to your computer, then print onto white cardstock.

Cut the strips apart and place inside your plastic eggs. I've also included a blank one, so that you can use any additional ideas you want to.

bit.ly/2aAQr4k

We always have a fun coded menu for our dinner that day. I choose a theme (i.e. Disney) and give the family a menu of crazy names. Everyone has to pick which items from the menu they want. All items end up being used. Sometimes they end up with things like a knife, water (no cup, so I bring a pitcher and pour it into their mouths), and Jell-o! I always use leftover party or holiday paper plates because you go through a lot!

Thomas Family | Texas

What comes to mind are some of the simple things we do that make our Easter Egg Hunt more organized, particularly for a larger family. For example, we color code the plastic eggs so when the "Easter Bunny" hides the eggs, it can be done according to age. Each child is given a color to hunt. This ensures that each person gets the same number of eggs, same candy, etc. I found it cuts down on the crying in the end. Also, every child gets to find a golden egg - which has money in it - coins, one dollar, or a five dollar bill. They always like that one.

The Savage Family

My in-laws celebrate March 4th, "Military Day", with us. We each receive a little gift in the mail every March 4th to remind us to "March Forth" in great ways. It's a little like New Year's Day when we "march forth" to do great things. I read, I think in a Family Fun Magazine, of a family that took it a "step" further. They had an old army boot that they spray painted gold. Every March 4th, each family member wrote a goal on a sheet of paper and put it in the boot, along with a dollar. The following year, the boot served as the centerpiece for dinner, and they pulled out the goals everyone had. The money inside was divided up among those who had accomplished their goal. Then they did it again for the following year.

The Pennock Family | Idaho

OPERATION: SUMMER KICKOFF FUN

I can't remember whose idea it was for a surprise water balloon fight, but it was brilliant. Especially since they didn't know it was coming!

It really took all of us to pull it off. My friends and I picked up the kids after school, and brought them to one central location. Just outside was a large green open space that was going to be where it all would happen. Two of us went out to the field to set things up. We had a cooler of water balloons for the kids too—we weren't going to leave them unarmed! Once the coolers were in place, they were ready and waiting in the field, hiding behind some trees and bushes, ready to make the first contact. Two of us, including me, stayed with the kids. We led them to the field and told them to be ready for a surprise. I'm not sure what they were expecting, but it certainly wasn't what happened next!

They rounded the corner, and water balloons started flying. You should have seen the kids' faces. There was a second of shock, and then it was on. I was laughing so hard, trying to hold my camera, throw water balloons, and try to avoid being hit, all at the same time. They found their water balloons quickly and soon it was an all out war. They were totally into it, and no side showed mercy . . . even for moms!

It turned out to be one of the most fun things we've done. We were soaking wet and couldn't stop laughing, and the kids LOVED it. I was cracking up at their comments . . .

"That was so unexpected!"

"That wasn't very ladylike."

"That was SO fun!"

Honestly, that was one of the most fun moments I've had with my kids, and to see their expressions when they realized what was happening? Totally priceless.

It cost next to nothing . . . the water balloons and ice cream for all of our kids was probably $10–$15. It doesn't have to cost a lot of money or take an immense amount of planning time to be something that your kids will remember. Simple has always been my mantra, and kids just love the together time. It's about creating moments that will last a lifetime.

This happened several years ago, and it was the start of our summer kickoff tradition. We love to celebrate the last day of school and our summer freedom, but we do something different each year, to change it up and try new things. We also can't do a surprise water balloon fight every year, because it wouldn't be a surprise!

This year it had finally been long enough that it was time for another surprise water balloon fight with new friends in our new town, and it was a smashing success. It's most definitely a family favorite.

· · · · · ·

I've gathered some other summer kickoff ideas that range from simple to some that take a little more planning. Most of them are very budget-conscious, and all of them will create a lasting memory!

1. Outdoor Movie Night

Hang up a white sheet or projector screen and enjoy a fun movie outdoors, with popcorn and other yummy treats! Invite neighbors and friends and make it a party!

2. Treasure Hunt

Hide fun summer items around your yard—goggles and other water gear, sidewalk chalk, bubbles—and leave clues for them to follow to find them.

3. Host a Tea Party

If you've got little girls, a tea party is always a fun idea. Let them each invite a friend or two, and they can make plans for the summer over yummy sandwiches and finger foods.

4. Night Games

Stay up late playing traditional night games with friends or neighbors . . . kick the can, ghost in the graveyard, capture the flag. These games bring back so many memories of my childhood! SO fun!

5. Pedicure Party

Bring out the summer polish colors, and have fun painting nails and getting toes ready for summer sandals!

6. Backyard Campout

Pitch a tent in the backyard, roast s'mores over the campfire, and sleep under the stars! Backyard camping is one of the easiest and fun ways to camp!

7. Appetizer and Bucket List Party

Make everyone's favorite appetizers, then make your family summer bucket list together while you're enjoying them.

8. Ice Cream and Summer Treats Bar

Make homemade ice cream, and break out all of the toppings and other favorite summer treats! Turn on the sprinklers, or jump in the pool—summer is here!

9. Movie Marathon

Older kids would love a movie marathon—all of the movies in one of their favorite series—plus popcorn and pizza, of course!

10. Summer Pen Pals

Help your kids find a summer pen pal, and write the first letter on the last day of school! Make envelopes out of scrapbook paper, and make a pen pal kit with fun pens, notebook, and stamps.

11. Library Run

Head to the library and stock up on fun summer books! You can start your at-home summer reading program the first day that school is out!

12. Popcorn Party

Lay out a popcorn bar—different flavors of popcorn and some cute brown lunch sacks for layering and mixing. Add in some yummy drinks and yard games like badminton and croquet, and you're set for fun!

13. Progressive BBQ

Join in with a few other families for a Progressive BBQ! Start at one house for appetizers and a game, head to the next home for the main event (hamburgers and hot dogs), then the last stop for dessert and even more games and fun. You could also do this at different fast food restaurants, maybe stopping at a fancier place for dessert!

A FUN SUMMER SCHEDULE

I thrive on a schedule and a regular routine, but I also love the freedom that summer provides, and spending lots of time with my kiddos. Let's be honest, don't we all look forward to that first week when school is out? We may not be sleeping in at our house (my kids are too little) but we can keep our pajamas on as long as we want, there are no lunches to pack or homework to do, and no schedule to follow. That lasts for about . . . a week. Then everything (and everyone) starts going crazy, and I start hearing the dreaded "I'm bored".

A few years ago I decided I needed a plan of action to make our everyday summer easier, run more smoothly, and be more FUN! They're only out for a couple of months, and I really wanted to make the most of our time together, without me going crazy, and without them feeling like there was nothing to do after the excitement of the first few weeks wore off.

I decided on a way to help keep them excited about each day, and give them something to look forward to. We tried it for the first time a few years ago and loved it. It's such an easy and fun plan! I assign each day with a specific theme or activity—Library Day, Baking Day, Water Day, Craft Day, and Exploration Day. It allows for everything we want to do, and the kids already know what to expect each day.

. . . . . .

MONDAY

This is the day we head to the library and read to our hearts' content, then bring home lots of books to enjoy throughout the week. The library is always a big part of our summer, and so is their reading program. We also do our own reading program at home, so books are a must.

TUESDAY

My kids love to bake, and so do I! We try new recipes and make our favorites, too. I think this is the perfect pajama day, don't you think?

WEDNESDAY

My kids love the water, so we really go at least 2–3 times a week to the pool or lake. I just like to try and have at least one per week, which is what the schedule is for. If it's rainy one week, our water day might be jumping in the puddles or on the wet trampoline!

THURSDAY

Crafts, crafts, crafts! My kids love to create, and I'm excited to have them start some new projects and fun crafts. It's not always a planned idea, and many times it's a when they pull out the crayons and paper, but sometimes I just pull out all the craft and art supplies and let them go to town.

FRIDAY

Exploration Day is the day we head out on an adventure! We look forward to exploring the area, visiting museums and zoos, discovering favorite parks, and going to the beach!

I really love having my kids at home, and incorporating this weekly schedule makes such a difference. Do we ALWAYS stick to it? No, of course not. Sometimes things come up, kids get sick, friends will invite us somewhere, there's an activity we want to attend on a different day, and plans may need to change. All of those things are to be expected, but that's okay. It's easy to switch days if we need to.

On the craft and baking days, I can do those in the morning or afternoon, depending on if we swim another day, or head out to another activity. We can certainly do more than one thing in a day, but we don't always. This is why I love it so much—it is a schedule, but with enough flexibility to make it easy to follow and still enjoy the freedom of summer.

The beauty of this idea is that you can easily tailor it to the needs of your family and ages of your kids. My kids are mostly small, so these are things that appeal to them. If you have teenagers, you can totally adjust the activities to what they want to do. Change the days, the activities, whatever works best for you.

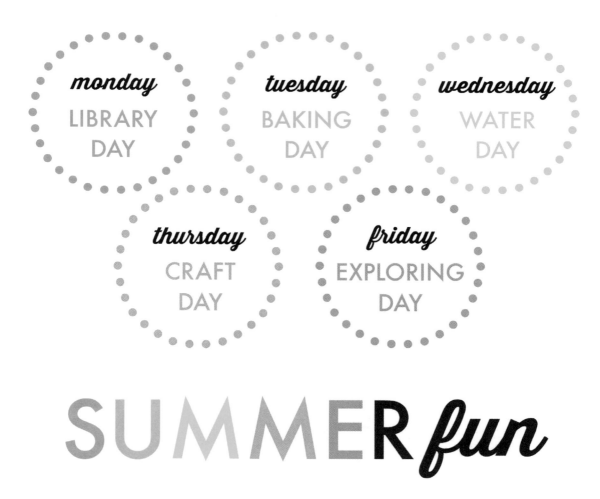

SUMMER BUCKET LIST

Oh, what do you do in the summertime?

Summer is the time to really enjoy our freedom, be spontaneous, and do things we just don't have the time to do as much of during the school year. Having more time with my kids is such a great thing, but it can also be challenging to keep them busy as the summer goes on, once the excitement of being out of school has rubbed off. Summer boredom can definitely occur at our house, and every year I try to put different plans in place to help prevent it, including a summer bucket list!

In addition to set activities that are written on the calendar, the bucket list includes activities that are for the most part ones that we can just pick up and do, without a lot of planning or effort ahead of time.

This gives my kids something to look forward to every day—after chores are done in the morning. I love it because it gives our summer a little more structure, while keeping some spontaneity at the same time. These activities aren't expensive or fancy, and many of them are things we do all year round, but something about doing them in the summertime makes them seem extra special! They're simple activities that all of us love, and really make summertime what it is.

When we create our summer bucket list, we sit down as a family and talk about all the things we really want to do, and each family member gets a chance to talk about their favorite activities. When we put them all down on paper, the result is a list we can refer to throughout the summer.

OUR SUMMER BUCKET LIST

· · · · · ·

- Put up the pool in the backyard
- Go to the beach
- Bake cookies
- Meet Dad for lunch
- Ride a carousel
- Feed the ducks
- Visit a museum
- Go bowling (www.kidsbowlfree.com)
- Family move night with concession stand
- Play outdoor night games (Kick the Can, anyone?)
- Go to the $1 movie
- Build a fort
- Have a pillow fight

- Play board games: Game night!
- Invite friends over for an ice cream party
- Go to the pool
- Put on a play or concert
- Visit the library
- Read stories together
- Have a water fight
- Sidewalk chalk!
- Play water games
- Run through the sprinklers
- Have a watermelon seed-spitting contest
- Go to storytime
- Individual lunch dates with each child

- Camping in the backyard
- S'mores Night
- Cereal night at the park
- Go hiking
- Visit the nature center
- Go to the fire station
- See a drive-in movie
- Have a lemonade stand
- Berry Picking
- Make homemade jam
- Watermelon spitting contest
- Make homemade bubbles
- Visit the fire station
- Go to your local fair
- Have a stargazing night, and look for shooting stars

We also have other activities that are specific to our area, and we love to explore where we live. We moved to upstate New York at the end of last summer, and our discovery list is long! You can do the same where you live—do some research and look online, talk to friends, check out books—figure out what there is to do within a reasonable distance, choose your favorites, and add them to the list!

When we are planning our week, we grab our summer bucket list, and plug in the things we want to do.

Several of the activities we will do more than one—maybe many times! It's really a guide, a starting point, and just gives everyone something to look forward to.

I love that they are simple activities that give us quality time together. I feel like the summertime is so short, I want to eek out every single moment with my kids that I can. It's important to remember that they don't have to be fancy, or take a lot of time and money to plan or prepare—it's just being together that counts!

WASHI TAPE SUMMER BUCKET

I've tried several different ways to keep track of our bucket list, but I really love this washi tape version. It's SO easy to make, and super cute too! It also doesn't take up too much space, and fits easily on a counter, shelf, or mantel. Here's how you make your own!

SUPPLIES

wooden craft sticks
washi tape
sharpie

DIRECTIONS

· Wrap a small piece of washi tape around the end of each craft stick—as many as sticks as you have bucket items!

· Use a fine tip Sharpie to write a bucket item on each stick, on the opposite end of the washi tape.

· Store your sticks in a half pint mason jar or other clear container with the words up. Turn the sticks over when you complete the bucket list item.

DOWNLOAD TAG

If you'd like the Summer Bucket List tag, enter the following link in the address bar of your computer. Save the file to your computer, then print onto white cardststock. I used a 2-inch circle punch to cut them out, and a little baker's twine to tie it onto my jar.

bit.ly/2aGjzH9

SUMMER READING PROGRAM

Reading has been a passion of mine since I could hold a book in my hand, and probably even before that. I remember as a young child going with my mom to our local library once a week in the summer, and poring over the shelves trying to discover a new book, and then searching for the next book in my current favorite series. I had a junior library card, and I was only able to check out ten books. I thought that was such a travesty—I was a fast reader, and those ten books only lasted a few days. I would read them again, and then beg my mom to take me back to the library before the full week was up.

The tooth fairy brought books to my house when you lost a tooth. In fact, she introduced me to many of the classics by the time I was eight or nine-years old. *Little Women, David Copperfield, Oliver Twist,* *Jane Eyre, Moby Dick, Wuthering Heights, Kidnapped, Treasure Island,* and *The Count of Monte Cristo* were just a few of my favorites. They were in a simplified form, of course, but I was hooked. Those same classics are still on my favorites list today.

Needless to say, I have always wanted to instill that same love of reading to my children, and having a Summer Reading Program is a great way to do it. It's also important for kids' literacy to continue reading throughout the summer when school is out, so they don't lose any of the progress they've made. If a child is struggling in this area—either needs to improve reading skills, or perhaps doesn't like to read—this reading program is a really great way to help motivate, encourage, and provide a little extra incentive.

· · · · · ·

HOW DOES IT WORK?

I created cute circle tags that say "I've read a book," and "I've read 20 minutes." (The download link is included below.) I have a small bucket for each child, and when they've completed either 20 minutes or have read one book, they take a circle and place it in their bucket. The specifics are all decided by age—my three readers use the 20-minute circles on a regular basis, and my little ones use the completed book circles. If my reading kids finish a book, they can add a book circle to their bucket for extra credit, but it has to be a chapter book that's on their reading level. The beauty of this program is that you can design it to be whatever you want and need it to be. Change it up to fit the needs and ages of your own children.

Each week I count the circles and award prizes for the totals. I want them to be able to earn something each week, with the prizes getting bigger as the weeks progress. The prize levels are different for each of my kids based on age, in order to even out the playing field.

Prizes can include:

Candy, trips to get ice cream, renting a movie, date night with mom or dad, a "staying up late" coupon, a special trip to the bookstore to choose a new book, a small toy, etc.

This can work for any age, and even my little ones can get in on the action, and have their own bucket. There are so many fabulous board books out there that are perfect for those chubby little hands, and they never get tired of hearing them over and over again. That's one of my favorite things about this program—regardless of the ages of your children, from toddlers on up to teenagers and adults—it's something for the entire family! You can absolutely adapt this program for the ages of your kids, and prizes that you'd like to incorporate.

DETAILS

Type the URL below into your browser. Save the PDF file to your computer, then print onto cute scrapbook paper or cardstock. Use a 2-inch circle punch (mine is by Fiskars) to punch them them out. I made a lot—based on the amount of kids I have, and how many circles I think they'll use. If you run out, you can always print more!

There are SO many wonderful books, I could have kept writing and listing them out for a long time, but there are some of our most beloved titles—the ones we come back to again and again.

CIRCLE TAGS DOWNLOAD

I READ 20 MINUTES:

bit.ly/2b1Uydp

I FINISHED A BOOK:

bit.ly/2aASc1y

FAVORITE CHAPTER BOOKS FOR GIRLS

- *Betsy & Tacy* (series) by Maud Hart Lovelace
- *All-of-a-Kind Family* by Sydney Taylor
- *Five Little Peppers and How They Grew* by Margaret Sidney
- *Little House on the Prairie* (and series) by Laura Ingalls Wilder
- *Anne of Green Gables* (series) by L.M. Montgomery
- *A Little Princess* by Frances Hodgson Burnett
- *Caddie Woodlawn* by Carol Ryrie Brink
- *Sarah, Plain and Tall* by Patricia MacLachlan
- *Hans Brinker, or The Silver Skates* by Mary Mapes Dodge
- *Pollyanna* by Eleanor H. Porter
- *Cotton in My Sack* by Lois Lenski
- *Strawberry Girl* by Lois Lenski
- *Peppermints in the Parlor* by Barbara Brooks Wallace
- *Nancy Drew* series (original) by Carolyn Keene
- *Trixie Belden* series by Julie Campbell
- *Cherry Ames* series by Helen Wells
- *The Boxcar Children* by Gertrude Chandler Warner
- *Tuesdays at the Castle* by Jessica Day George
- *Princess Academy* by Shannon Hale
- *The Hundred Dresses* by Eleanor Estes

FAVORITE CHAPTER BOOKS FOR BOYS

- *The Great Brain* by John D. Fitzgerald
- *Encyclopedia Brown, Boy Detective* by Donald J. Sobol
- *The Dark is Rising (sequence of five books)* by Susan Cooper
- *Fablehaven series* by Brandon Mull
- *Harry Potter series* by J.K. Rowling
- *Percy Jackson series* by Rick Riordan
- *The Mouse and the Motorcycle* by Beverly Clearly
- *The Indian in the Cupboard* by Lynne Reid Banks
- *The Adventures of Tom Sawyer* by Mark Twain
- *Call Me Francis Tucket (series)* by Gary Paulsen
- *The Lion, the Witch, and the Wardrobe (series)* by C.S. Lewis
- *Treasure Island (Sterling Illustrated Classics)* by Robert Louis Stevenson
- *20,000 Leagues Under the Sea* by Jules Verne
- *The Call of the Wild* by Jack London
- *The Westing Game* by Ellen Raskin

FAVORITE CHILDREN'S BOOKS

- *Sheila Rae the Brave* by Kevin Henkes
- *Bread and Jam for Frances (and all Frances books)* by Russell & Lillian Hoban
- *The Story of Ferdinand* by Munro Leaf
- *Sylvester and the Magic Pebble* by William Steig
- *Blueberries for Sal* by Robert McCloskey
- *Little Bear* by Elsa Holmelund Minarik
- *Frog & Toad* by Arnold Lobel
- *Tikki Tikki Tembo* by Arlene Mosel
- *Strega Nona* by Tomie dePaola
- *The Snowy Day* by Ezra Jack Keats
- *Where the Wild Things Are* by Maurice Sendak
- *Madeline* by Ludwig Bemelmans
- *Chicken Soup with Rice* by Maurice Sendak
- *The Paper Bag Princess* by Robert Munsch
- *Caps for Sale* by Esphyr Slobodkina
- *Amelia Bedelia* by Peggy Parish
- *Magic School Bus (series)* by Joanna Cole
- *The Tale of Peter Rabbit* by Beatrix Potter
- *If you Give a Mouse a Cookie* by Laura Numeroff
- *The Going to Bed Book* by Sandra Boynton
- *The Very Hungry Caterpillar* by Eric Carle

- *We're Going on a Bear Hunt* by Michael Rosen
- *Jamberry* by Bruce Degen
- *Skip to My Lou* by Nadine Bernard Westcott
- *The Little Mouse, The Red Ripe Strawberry and The Big, Hungry Bear* by Don & Audrey Wood
- *Big, Red Barn* by Margaret Wise Brown
- *The Runaway Bunny* by Margaret Wise Brown
- *Good Night, Gorilla* by Peggy Rathmann
- *Moo, Baa, La La La* by Sandra Boynton
- *Pajama Time* by Sandra Boynton
- *Chicka Chicka Boom Boom* by Bill Martin, Jr.
- *Sheep in a Jeep* by Nancy Shaw
- *Barnyard Dance* by Sandra Boynton
- *Brown Bear, Brown Bear* by Eric Carle
- *Goodnight Moon* by Margaret Wise Brown
- *Tumble Bumble* by Felicia Bond
- *Mike Mulligan and his Steam Shovel* by Virginia Lee Burton
- *Little Blue Truck* by Alice Schertle and Jill McElmurry
- *From Head to Toe* by Eric Carle
- *The Carrot Seed* by Ruth Krauss
- *A Mother for Choco* by Keiki Kasza
- *Go, Dog, Go!* by P.D. Eastman
- *Guess How Much I Love You* by Sam McBratney and Anita Jeram
- *What's Up, Duck?* by Tad Hills

MOVIE NIGHT & CONCESSION STAND

Family movie nights have always been a regular part of our week. Whenever it fits into the schedule that week, we love to snuggle up on the couch or in our bed to watch a movie and eat popcorn. We love being all together, in such close proximity—usually laughing and making little comments along the way.

Once in a while I'll do a concession stand for our movie night, which the kids absolutely love, and is a special treat. One of my close friends introduced me to it years ago, and I loved it so much I immediately incorporated it into our own family. While we do it throughout the year, it's one of my kids' absolute favorite end-of-summer traditions.

The entire week leading up to our movie night, the kids are able to earn "money" (I use Monopoly money or plastic tokens) by making good choices, being kind to siblings, listening right away to mom and dad, going the extra mile, and getting all of their jobs done.

The night of the movie, I set up the concession stand with a variety of items and label them with a price—bags of popcorn, candy bars, bottled water and lemonade, cookies, and fruit (which is free!).

Before I price the items, I look to see how much the kids earned, so I can coordinate the prices accordingly. If they've only earned $5, I don't want to put the prices too high, and if they've earned $20 I don't put everything at $1 or $2, or they'll end up with way too many sweets.

About ten minutes before we start the movie, the kids get to come to the concession stand and use their earned money from the week to purchase the treats that they want to eat while we watch our movie. It is so fun to see them get so excited about everything that's there, and the fact that they earned it themselves.

Not only is it a really fun family tradition, it also encourages extra good behavior that week. Sometimes when we need a little "kickstart" to improve our good choices, a concession stand is a great way to start.

I like to keep it as a special activity, so we only do it a handful of times each year, but ending the summer and kicking off the new school year has always been the perfect time to do it!

· · · · · ·

To surprise family members on their birthdays we stay up late the night before or arise early in the morning and sneakily decorate the breakfast table and kitchen in a fun way that the celebrated person will love. This includes balloons, napkins shaped into butterflies, hanging lanterns, homemade notes and cards, and, of course, their favorite breakfast. We have fun working and planning creatively to honor one another.

The Schmitt Family | Massachusetts

HOMEMADE ICE CREAM

When I think of 4th of July's past, there's one thing in particular that's always been a part of it—homemade ice cream. I can't even remember an Independence Day of my childhood without it.

When I think about it, I can hear the whir of the ice cream machine, and all of our voices as we asked my mom a million times when it would be ready. 45 minutes never seemed so long! I can smell the sweet aroma of vanilla, because that was our favorite flavor. Finally, it was ready, and we would carry our bowls out to the front porch to eat it while we waited for the fireworks to start. I thought life just couldn't be any better than that moment.

Food often evokes the strongest memories, and they connect us to certain events, holidays, and people.

Homemade ice cream is a part of my childhood—a 4th of July tradition that I knew I wanted to carry on to my own family.

Now my kids are the ones clamoring to know when the ice cream will be done, and I love making it for them. It's still a part of our 4th of July, and we all love it!

There are many recipes for homemade vanilla ice cream, but I have one that I love the very most. It's very simple—just milk, cream, sugar, vanilla, and a little salt—but it's easy to make, and the taste is divine! You can add whatever mix-ins you like, from chocolate to fruit—or even just put out the toppings after the ice cream is finished, and let people choose their own.

. . . . . .

INGREDIENTS

2½ cups whole milk
2½ cups sugar
½ tsp. salt
2½ cups half and half
1½ Tbsp. vanilla
5 cups whipping cream

DIRECTIONS

· Mix all the ingredients together and pour into your ice cream maker. Freeze as directed (you will need ice and rock salt).

· If I'm making something other than vanilla, and using mix-ins, I start the ice cream maker and let it thicken, then I add my fruit/cookies/candy pieces, and let it finish freezing.

· If you don't have an ice cream maker, there are some other ways to make it that are super fun for kids to help with! Even if you do have one, these are so fun, you might want to try them anyway!

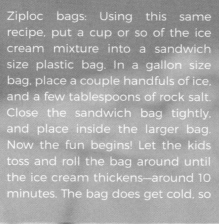

Ziploc bags: Using this same recipe, put a cup or so of the ice cream mixture into a sandwich size plastic bag. In a gallon size bag, place a couple handfuls of ice, and a few tablespoons of rock salt. Close the sandwich bag tightly, and place inside the larger bag. Now the fun begins! Let the kids toss and roll the bag around until the ice cream thickens—around 10 minutes. The bag does get cold, so you may want to hold it with a towel.

Cans: Cans work too! You will need two different sized cans—both with lids. A #10 can, and smaller coffee cans work well. Your ice cream will go in the smaller can, and then placed inside the #10 can. Add the ice and rock salt around the smaller can, then seal with the lid. Roll the can around until you have ice cream!

Photography Credit—www.yourhomebasedmom.com

GOING TO SEE A DRIVE-IN MOVIE

There are so many reasons we love going to a drive-in movie as a family. There's just something about sitting in the back of the truck, snuggling up in blankets, and munching on popcorn while you watch a giant screen with the big, dark sky and twinkling stars as a backdrop.

It's also a tie to the past, and as an old-fashioned girl, I love anything that speaks of history. I was so excited to introduce it to my kids for the first time, and I wasn't disappointed. It was most definitely one of the highlights of the summer, and it was quickly decided that it would be one of our summer traditions from that point forward.

· · · · · ·

Why our family loves the drive-in movie

· If you're taking kids, they don't have to be as quiet as church mice. One of the hardest things about taking little kids to a theater is helping them learn how to whisper when they have to go to the bathroom, get a drink, or have a comment/question about the movie. That is a huge plus in my book!

· It's more social! It's more like watching a movie at your house than a theater, because you can have a little more of a conversation (if you want to).

· It's usually quite a but cheaper, and often children of certain ages are admitted free of charge. Every drive-in will be different, but at ours, children ages 5–12 are only $5, and 4 and under are free. That makes it a lot more reasonable to go to a movie as a family!

· You get to see more than one movie with double and even triple features! Most drive-ins will have a double or triple feature, so by paying one price, you get to see more than one movie. Can't beat that!

· You can bring lots of blankets and pillows, snuggle up, and get pretty comfy. When babies or smallest children fall asleep, they can be tucked in cozily while everyone else enjoys the evening, especially if you're staying for a double or triple feature.

· You can bring your own food—everything from snacks and drinks to a full meal! There are usually concession stands if you want to buy there, but I love being able to bring all of our favorites AND it saves a ton of money at the same time.

Tips for reducing stress and having fun

· Do all the research you can ahead of time about the theater, and what the rules are. Each drive-in can be different, so even if you've been to one before, still check before you go. Hopefully they have a website or Facebook page you can get information from, but if not, you may need to give them a call. I also signed up for our theater's newsletter, so I get the lineup of movies every week. It makes it easy for me to look at our schedule and see if it's something we want to do and can do.

· Arrive early, especially on a weekend. You want to be at the front of that line of cars, not the back! Even if you get in early, you can eat, talk, play games, and hang out until the movie starts, plus you'll get a much better parking spot.

· Consider going during the week, instead of on the weekend. If you can fit it in Monday-Thursday, the crowds are almost certain to be less, and it might be easier to manage with little kids.

· At our drive-in, you tune into a certain frequency on the radio in order to hear the movie, but you can also bring battery-powered portable radios to listen to outside of the car. Decide how you want to do it ahead of time, or just bring along a radio just in case.

- Know where the bathrooms are as soon as you arrive. I don't know about you, but we seem to have a bathroom emergency just about everywhere we go!

To find drive-in theaters in your area, check out this website:

www.driveintheater.com/drivlist.htm

If you don't have one near you, try having your own at home! Look into renting or borrowing a projector, hang a big, white sheet on one side of your house or garage, and you'll have the perfect outdoor movie without leaving your own home!

FLASHLIGHT TAG & NIGHT GAMES

There is just something about playing games outside at night. I remember as a child and teenager being outside in our street or in our yard, running around, playing, and laughing until our sides hurt. I have loved night games ever since, into both my college and now adult years. It's something I've always wanted to do with my kids—to pass along these games that perhaps in this digital world we live in have become a bit old-fashioned. We love to put away all the electronics and enjoy being together outside. Summer isn't summer without night games!

We started playing flashlight tag with our kids even when they were very small, and it is a family favorite. We have Family Night one night a week, and this is one of the most requested activities ever! If it's summer, we play outside, but during the long winters we can play it inside as well.

Oh my goodness, the laughter! We team everyone up (the smallest with mom and dad), round up enough flashlights for everyone, and then start to play. Negotiations to stay up later and play a little longer always start coming when we give them the five-minute warning, and we usually give in, because my husband and I love it too!

There are some other really fun night games on my list too—some of them are best played with older children and teenagers, but most of them can be adapted so that the whole family can play together, even the youngest ones!

It's so fun to have friends and other families over to join you—it's a great way to establish new friendships and deepen others. Play games, eat treats, and enjoy the night! What about your neighbors? Meet in the street and play—it can be a neighborhood tradition!

· · · · · ·

FLASHLIGHT TAG

It's basically a combination of hide-and-seek and tag. Separate into teams, and then pass out flashlights for each team. One of the teams is "it", and counts to a specified number while all the other teams go and hide. When the "it" team finishes counting, they try to find the other teams. You're "caught" when the beam of the light flashes on your faces! Repeat until all teams are caught, then start again!

KICK-THE-CAN

This is a classic night game, and there are several variations that have appeared over the years, but basically you need at least 3-4 people (and even more make it more fun!), a can, a place for a "jail" within sight of the can, and plenty of space to run around. One person is deemed "it" and they put one foot on the can while they count to a specified number, while everyone else goes and hides. When they finish counting, they start looking for everyone else, while keeping one eye on the can. The players that were hiding try to get past the person that's it and kick the can. If they're tagged before they can, then they go to jail. The person that's it wins if he/she can tag all the players and send them to jail. If the can is kicked, all players are released from jail.

CAPTURE THE FLAG

This game is even more fun played at night! You need two teams—at least a total of six players, but the more the better. Divide a large playing field/area in half—as equally as you can, and clearly mark the boundaries. Each team has a side, and they hide a "flag" somewhere where at least a portion of it is visible.

Photography credit—www.ccmcafeeperspective.com

Once the game starts, the teams each try to capture the other's flag, and make it back to their own side without being caught. If a player is tagged on the other team's side, they go to their jail. They can be released from jail if one of their fellow players makes it over and tags them without being caught—then they both get to walk back across to their own side safely. The first team to capture the other team's flag wins!

GHOST IN THE GRAVEYARD

To start, designate one person as the "ghost" and a base that's "safe". You'll also want to establish the hiding boundaries. The ghost then goes and hides while all the other players count to a specified number. Then they go and look for the ghost. The player that finds the ghost yells "GHOST IN THE GRAVEYARD" to warn all the other players. That player is also safe, but all the other players have to make it back to the designated base before the ghost tags them. The first person is tagged becomes the ghost for the next game.

CEREAL NIGHT AT THE PARK

When my second set of twins was born, my girls, the first set had just turned three-years old, and I had five little kids at home. My husband was very busy at work at the time, and most nights I was on my own for dinner with the kids. It got a little . . . hectic sometimes, and I just didn't always have the time or energy to make dinner.

We all love cereal at our house, and my kids especially love sugar cereal—which I never buy except on very special occasions. On several of these nights when my husband was gone, it would be a "cereal night," and that would be dinner. One particular night when my twin boys were around 18-months old, the kids were especially antsy and needed to get out of the house, but we still needed dinner, so Cereal Night at the Park was born!

I packed them all up in the truck, and we headed to the grocery store. They got to pick out ANY kind of cereal they wanted, which basically felt like Christmas to them. I think we spent a good twenty minutes in the cereal aisle, because they just couldn't decide which one they wanted most. Finally, we had cereal, milk, plastic spoons, and paper bowls in our cart, and we were ready to check out.

I took them to one of our favorite parks, set out the milk and cereal, and they went to town. After they ate, they played until dark, and it ended up being one of our favorite nights of the summer. A tradition was also born, and at least once during the summer months, we have Cereal Night at the Park!

We love this night for many reasons, and it's easy to either plan, or do spontaneously. It's a great night to try out a new park, and see if you can find a new favorite.

· · · · · ·

THE BEST CHEWY CARAMEL POPCORN

Popcorn is like another food group at our house, and there aren't many nights that go by where someone isn't asking if we can make some. I think my oldest son is made of half popcorn!

We love it the traditional way, but adding caramel is just another yummy and delicious way to enjoy it. Our summer movie nights almost always include popcorn, and this recipe makes a frequent appearance.

To make the caramel, you need a candy thermometer. If you don't have one, you can get one pretty inexpensively just about anywhere—but make sure it's for candy, and not meat. You can also try the cold-water method instead (put a little bit of the mixture into a cup of cold water to see how firm it is), but I think it's a lot trickier to get right if you haven't done it a lot.

This recipe only takes about 10 minutes to make, but it's easy—just add the ingredients and stir while cooking! I prefer to use air popped popcorn, but if you don't have a popcorn popper, you can use microwave popcorn instead. It will have a slightly different taste, but it's still good. If you love chewy, gooey popcorn, this recipes is for you!

. . . . . .

INGREDIENTS

1 cup brown sugar
¾ cup granulated sugar
½ cup butter
14 oz. can sweetened
   condensed milk
1½ cups corn syrup
16 cups popped popcorn

DIRECTIONS

· Combine all ingredients (except popcorn) in large, heavy saucepan. Bring to a boil over medium heat, making sure to STIR constantly or it will burn!

· Keep stirring as it boils until it reaches the soft ball stage, 234 degrees on your candy thermometer. Remove from heat, and immediately pour over the popcorn. Stir until coated. Let cool, then enjoy!

BERRY PICKING

Michigan summers are the absolute best. We spent twelve wonderful years living there, starting with graduate school and then our first job. Most of our children were born there, as well as many of our family traditions. We went berry picking for the first time our very first summer there, and it's been one of our favorite summer traditions ever since. When we moved to Texas a couple of years ago, we were fortunate to be able to continue the tradition, and now in upstate New York as well.

We've picked blueberries, blackberries, and strawberries, and we all have a berry we like best. We eat a ton of them pretty much immediately, and the ones that survive go into things like homemade jam, specialty pancakes and baked goods, smoothies, and milkshakes. We also freeze some to eat later, and I love being able to go to the freezer even in the dead of winter and pull some out for a batch of berry muffins.

The actual picking is always an adventure. We choose family-friendly berry farms that encourage kids to pick too, and they love having their very own bucket—even the littlest ones. Picking blueberries means eating them as you go (per the farm okay), and one of my favorite memories of my one year old twin boys is seeing them in their stroller, picking blueberries as fast as they could, and stuffing them in their mouths.

One of our favorite times to pick berries is on family night, which for our family is Monday night, and we set it aside each week to spend time together as a family. We often have friends join us, which is always fun! Berry picking night also means ice cream or Slurpees afterward, and I'm pretty sure that's just as eagerly anticipated!

We've also had a few minor incidents over the years, and one of them will probably live in infamy. On one summer blueberry-picking trip, we ended up picking more than we ever had before—I don't know how many pounds it was, but just by looking at our buckets, we knew we had a lot. When we were finished, we packed up the car, and started over to the main stand to get them weighed and pay for them. As we were backing up, we heard a sickening crunch, and our hearts sunk. Sure enough, the bucket had accidentally been left behind one of the tires, and all of our berries were smashed all over the ground. The bucket was also beyond repair. It was the saddest moment, and we picked up the bucket remnants and headed over to tell the farm what happened, and to pay for them.

They laughed so hard, felt so sorry for us, and didn't even have us pay for them! We moved away from Michigan soon after, and that ended up being the last summer picking at that farm. The next summer we got a phone call from some of our best friends, and they told us that "our bucket" was hanging up in the farm stand, with my husband's name on it, as a funny warning to customers! We have been laughing about it ever since.

This year was our first year picking strawberries here in upstate New York, and oh how yummy they were! I don't know how we got so lucky, but the berry farm is literally two miles down the road from our house. We live in the country, and I guess it's one of the perks! It was a perfect summer evening, and we enjoyed picking berries, watching the farm animals, chatting with new friends, and just being outside together.

Berry picking is a wonderful family activity, and just really FUN. It provides a lot of time for talking, laughing, and spending quality time together. You also get a lot of fresh, yummy fruit, for things like jam, and a plethora of unforgettable memories.

. . . . . .

HOMEMADE JAM

I first made jam with a good friend of mine when my oldest son was around three years old. We were pretty new to our town, and she had been so kind to me, and helped get acclimated to our area. She invited me over to help, and even though I had never canned anything in my life, I wanted to give it a try.

We lived in Michigan at the time, and berries are bounteous in the summers there. You could pick your own (like we did), or get them at Farmer's Markets that had great prices.

I had been so intimidated when we first started, and by the end of that day, I had learned a skill as well as confidence that I could do it on my own. When my family and I tasted the jam that we made, we were hooked. Now, whenever we pick berries, homemade jam is always on the list!

Most of the time I do freezer jam, because it's super fast and super easy. Cooked jam isn't hard, but there are more steps and more equipment needed. I always use the recipe on the back of the Sure-Jell (pectin) box, and we love it. There is a light version too, if you want to use less sugar! I also follow the Sure-Jell recipe if I'm doing cooked jam.

Jam is a perfect family activity. Kids love to help mash the fruit, and help stir while it's cooking. Getting everyone in the kitchen together is a wonderful way to spend some really great quality time together, and teach a skill at the same time. I've discovered that being in the kitchen together as a family—answering questions, letting them help, and listening to them talk has been one of the most valuable times together we've had. It doesn't matter what you're making— just that you're doing it together!

If you love to give homemade made gifts, jam is one of the best! Make it in the summer or fall, and have it ready for Christmas and holiday gifts. Tie a festive ribbon around the rim, and add a cute printable on top, and you've got a lovely gift for neighbors, friends, teachers, and anyone else on your list! Or give it anytime—there doesn't even need to be a reason other than brightening someone's day.

. . . . . .

DETAILS

I've created a darling printable that's perfect for the top of your homemade jam jars! Just type in one of the URL addresses below, and save the PDF file to your computer. Print it on cardstock (I like the brown kraft paper cardstock), and then use a 2 inch circle punch to cut them out. Adhere with double stick tape. You can also punch a hole in the top and tie it on with a ribbon instead.

BLACKBERRY JAM
bit.ly/2b9IUA4

PEACH JAM
bit.ly/2aWH5kf

RASPBERRY JAM
bit.ly/2b9mqhv

STRAWBERRY JAM
bit.ly/2b9dTb6

strawberry
jam

homemade with love . homemade with love . homemade with love . homemade with love .

CAMPING IN THE BACKYARD

Camping is a fabulous part of our summer. We relish the outdoors, and completely enjoy being surrounded by and exploring nature. I love letting the kids loose, and watching them run, skip rocks, play with sticks, build makeshift forts, and absolutely have the time of their lives. Just the thought of Dutch oven potatoes and peach, the vision of the starry night sky, and the deliciously smoky smell of the campfire are enough to get me ready to go!

One of our favorite ways to go camping keeps us very close to home . . . and in the backyard! I have pictures of my oldest son, peeking his darling, tiny little face outside the tent as we set up the brand new tent my husband received from my parents as a graduation gift. We were thrilled, and knew the perfect way to inaugurate it was by a backyard campout. That tradition has stayed with us, and at least once every summer, we have a backyard campout.

It's really a perfect arrangement when you don't have time to leave for a few days, plus you don't have to pack! Just throw up your tent in the backyard, bring out sleeping bags or pillows and blankets, and you're just about ready. It can be planned, or it can be spontaneous, which is sometimes even more fun. I also love that the bathroom is close, and when I had a small baby, we both could sleep inside after everyone else was tucked in for the night.

Lots of activities go along with our backyard campouts, and some of our favorites include s'mores and scary stories around the campfire, homemade ice cream, badminton, croquet, bocce ball, flashlight tag, card games, and nighttime hide and seek a.k.a. ghosts in the graveyard. We usually turn on a movie inside the tent when we're ready for the kids to calm down, and snuggling down inside our sleeping bags with a big bowl of popcorn is the perfect way to end the night before drifting off to sleep.

When morning comes (usually really early, when the sun rises), it's inside the house for pancakes and orange juice—a yummy ending to our backyard campout. We try and do it more than once during the summer, and even into the fall, but it's always at least once!

These nights create so many memories, and it's a simple, inexpensive way to connect with your kids and spend some quality time together.

· · · · · ·

S'MORES RECIPE

Campfires are synonymous with summer at our house. We've built one in every home we've owned, and nothing says a summer night like sitting out under the stars and night sky around a crackling fire. They are always a part of our backyard campouts!

Most of the time we make them the original way: marshmallows, chocolate, and graham crackers, but not always! Having a S'mores night is the perfect way to get a little crazy and experiment with other ways to make them. It's also a great excuse to invite a few friends over to enjoy them with! Have everyone bring a different ingredient to try, and then take a vote about which one you all like best. It's so fun for kids and adults alike!

· · · · · · ·

Some ideas for Hershey's chocolate substitutions:
· Reese's PB Cups

· Snickers

· Kit Kat

· Twix

· Three Musketeers

Or sub out the graham crackers instead and use:
· Peanut butter cookies

· Chocolate chip cookies

· Nutter Butter cookies

· Oreos

You can also make a dip by melting marshmallows over the chocolate, and dipping graham crackers, prezels, or other bite-size cookies. If you don't have a fire pit, you can also make them over a gas burner on your stove, or even in the microwave. What's important are the ingredients . . . and most of all, the people!

ABOUT THE AUTHOR

Kierste Wade is the author of Simply Kierste, a DIY & Lifestyle blog, where she has been sharing creative ideas since 2009. As the mother of six, she loves to feature simple ideas for both home and family, including organization, holiday traditions and activities, home décor, DIY, recipes, printables, and more. Her work has been featured in many publications, both online and in print, including CountryLiving.com, HGTV.com, Parents.com, and Babycenter.com. She's happy to make her home in upstate New York with her family in their farmhouse, Old Salt Farm.

ACKNOWLEDGMENTS

I am so grateful for the opportunity to write this book, and to write about something that I love so much and is such an integral part of our family. Traditions have brought so much joy into our home that I really wanted to share that with all of you.

I've learned a lot through the book writing process, not only about myself, but also about how much support and love I have from my family and friends. I feel so lucky to have so many wonderful people in my life, and I would be remiss if I didn't relay my gratitude to them.

My dear husband is a saint—or about as close as you can get. He filled my shoes often while I was busy creating, writing, editing, and taking photos, pulling double duty without complaint. My children didn't complain (too much) about eating cereal for dinner a little more often than usual, and loved celebrating Easter in July and Christmas in October, because writing this book did not line up perfectly with the holidays. I did have to laugh at the look on the postal worker's face when I took Easter Eggs to the post office in mid-summer to be mailed to my kids! I love this family of mine, and I simply could not have done it without them.

My parents passed on their love of tradition, especially my mom, and I'm grateful for the childhood they gave me and my siblings. My mom also helped me with editing, and she was there whenever I needed her. My sister was an earpiece throughout the process, and I knew I could always call on her. And my friends? I am so thankful for the words of encouragement, support, and motivation, and for the calls, texts, emails and social media shout-outs. How I got so lucky, I'll never know, but I hope they all know how much I love and appreciate each one of them. I feel the same about my Simply Kierste readers—and thank them to the bottom of my heart for their support!

· · · · · ·